THE
FINALISTS II

EXCERPTS FROM THE FIVE 2007
COSTA AWARD-WINNING BOOKS

Published by C

The Finalists II:
Excerpts from the five 2007 Costa Award-winning books

First published in Great Britain in 2007 by
Costa Publishing
Whitbread PLC
Whitbread Court
Houghton Hall Business Park
Porz Avenue
Dunstable
Bedfordshire LU5 5XE

A CIP catalogue record for this book is available from the British Library.

ISBN 978-0-9554863-1-9

Designed and typeset in Trade Gothic and Adobe Garamond by Meteorite.
Printed in Great Britain by Lamport Gilbert Limited, 3 Darwin Close, Reading,
Berkshire RG2 0TB.

INTRODUCTION

There's nothing quite like relaxing with a good book and a cup of coffee, and I'm therefore delighted to be able to invite you to sit back and enjoy a bite-sized preview of the five winners of this year's Costa Book Awards.

One of the UK's most prestigious and popular book prizes, the Costa (formerly the Whitbread) Book Awards have, since 1971, honoured some of the best books of the year by writers based in the UK or Ireland.

From 553 books entered this year, our hard-working judging panels have selected five Award Winners across five categories – a novel, a first novel, a biography, a children's book and a collection of poetry.

We're also delighted to feature the winning short story from the competition we sponsored in Woman & Home magazine this year.

Recapturing past happiness; a shocking disappearance; astonishing new evidence about a dictator's childhood; poems describing a world in free-fall; life through the eyes of a twelve year old; and a story about a mysterious handyman...

Six fantastic reasons to linger a little longer at your local Costa. Lose yourself in these stunning pieces of writing and meet the fascinating, frightening and fabulous characters that inhabit this collection of some of the finest books of 2007.

All proceeds from the sale of The Finalists II will be donated directly to the Costa Foundation. Read more overleaf to see how your contribution will make a difference.

John Derkach
Managing Director, Costa

Visit the website at **www.costabookawards.com**

THE COSTA FOUNDATION

The Costa Foundation was set up in 2006 to give something directly back to Costa's coffee producers.

Since the beginning of 2007 we've been developing and implementing programmes to improve the social and economic welfare of communities in Colombia, Uganda and Ethiopia.

Through a donation directly from Costa, and fundraising across all UK stores, the Costa Foundation has invested in education, better sanitation and developed land for crop-growing.

Education has been identified as a key driver of healthy communities. So the Foundation's focus in 2007 has been the communities where children had to walk as far as 10km to school or where there was no clean water.

In Anatoli School in Colombia, a new school has been built, with six classrooms, a computer and internet room, cafeteria and library, and in December, over 200 children moved into the completed school.

And to support the whole family, we've also developed a fish and poultry farm as well as a plot of land for growing crops.

In Mushasha, Uganda, children will soon be able to take their classes in a newly-built school and in Rwemigango, the project includes replacing three structurally unsound classrooms. When both these schools are finished, 160 rural children will benefit – with a 78% increase in those able to go to school.

We've also raised funds for four new teachers, two new classroom blocks and two new teachers' houses, as well as providing all the school equipment. In addition, we're improving the sanitation and installing four water tanks for water harvesting.

THE COSTA FOUNDATION

In Kilenso Rasa School in Ethiopia, we're building a new secondary school to accommodate 480 children from four schools in 12 parishes. Eight new classrooms and a library are being built and furnished for the children.

This is a major achievement when considering that 83% of students used to leave after junior school. Soon, for the first time, they will have a secondary school to go to.

All of the proceeds from the sale of The Finalists II will help to fund similar projects in our coffee-growing communities and we would like to take this opportunity to thank you for your support.

If you would like to find out more about the projects supported by the Costa Foundation, or would like to make a further donation, please visit **www.thecostafoundation.org**

COSTA FOUNDATION

HELPING COMMUNITIES GROW

SIX BOOK CHALLENGE

The Costa Book Awards is delighted to sponsor the Six Book Challenge™.

This national initiative to support less confident adult readers takes place from January to May 2008 and invites people to read six books whilst supporting them with incentives and creative reading activities.

Co-ordinated by The Reading Agency, the Challenge is being run by public libraries in partnership with local learning providers.

For more information, visit **www.sixbookchallenge.org.uk**.

CONTENTS

The Handyman by Jenny Steel
Copyright © 2007 by Jenny Steel

The Bower Bird by Ann Kelley
Copyright © 2007 by Ann Kelley
First published in 2007 by Luath Press Limited, Edinburgh.
www.luath.co.uk

What Was Lost by Catherine O'Flynn
Copyright © 2007 by Catherine O'Flynn
First published in January in 2007 by Tindal Street Press Ltd,
217 The Custard Factory, Gibb Street, Birmingham, B9 4AA.
www.tindalstreet.co.uk

Young Stalin by Simon Sebag Montefiore
Copyright © 2007 Simon Sebag Montefiore
First published in Great Britain in 2007 by Weidenfeld & Nicolson,
The Orion Publishing Group Ltd, Orion House,
5 Upper Saint Martin's Lane, London, WC2H 9EA.
www.orionbooks.co.uk

Tilt by Jean Sprackland
Copyright © 2007 by Jean Sprackland
First published in Great Britain in 2007 by Jonathan Cape,
Random House, 20 Vauxhall Bridge Road, London SW1V 2SA.
www.randomhouse.co.uk

Day by A. L. Kennedy
Copyright © 2007 by A.L. Kennedy
First published in Great Britain in 2007 by Jonathan Cape,
Random House, 20 Vauxhall Bridge Road, London SW1V 2SA.
www.randomhouse.co.uk

THE HANDYMAN

by **Jenny Steel**

Winner of the 2007 Woman & Home Short Story
Competition, sponsored by Costa

THE HANDYMAN

by **Jenny Steel**

The Handyman tells the story of Betty, who advertises for a handyman. When kind, gentle Mr Jones turns up on her doorstep he seems perfect, but Betty's daughter Stella is not convinced.

Jenny Steel, *a retired teacher, won the Woman & Home Short Story Competition. She lives in Bredon, Gloucestershire, with her husband Richard. They have three grown-up children and three grandchildren.*

The judges were bowled over by Jenny's controlled style and evocative language. **"It was so poignant and beautifully written, and it ended on such a satisfying note."**

THE HANDYMAN

STELLA WAS, is my first-born and only child. Since her father's death, she has chosen to monitor my wellbeing via weekly phone calls, a chore made easier by the knowledge that I am as I have always been, 'fine'. Any suggestion of inadequacy would threaten our mutual independence.

For my part, I choose to answer her calls and her questions while in the security of my sitting-room, a space pleasing to my eye, made comfortable by my own hand, echoing as it does the colours and patterns of the garden.

It was from here that I chose to let her know of the small change I had made to my circumstances.

'Oh, by the way, dear, I've found a handyman at last.'

Silence.

'What do you mean "found"?'

'Usual channels – you know, word of mouth, ' I lied, thinking of him standing on my doorstep, holding the postcard that had long been pinned on the post office board.

'What about references?'

I had named her Stella in the hope of liberating her from the conventional family mould, but at forty she was still, as she had always been, a disappointingly pedantic child.

'Immaculate.' For this was how I assessed my own judgment of the man who had presented himself.

Dressed in the colours of the earth and seasons, his tweed jacket, moleskin trousers and working shirt were of stiff material, grown comfortable with age, as indeed had he. Ash-handled tools, patinated with use and care, arranged in a roughened leather pannier were eloquent in their recommendation of this working man.

'Where does he come from?'

I suppressed the desire to shock with a literal truth.

'He's local. I've seen him around. He rides a bicycle. Oh, and another thing – it could be an advantage ...' I had thought about attempting a light laugh, '... he doesn't speak ...or hear.'

With my free hand, I twisted a wilting blossom from the pale pink red cyclamen on my writing table. Responding mechanically to the expected, blustering cautions, I recalled to mind the few fluttering and cupping movements of his huge hands with which he had conveyed his silent world.

'I promise you that it is not a problem. We can communicate very well.'

And so it was that Joseph Jones came into my life.

Our contract was set in accordance with the few terms I had suggested on the postcard.

Each Tuesday and Thursday he would arrive promptly at 9.30am and work as needed in the house or garden for three hours. He was to be paid by cheque each week. Extra expenses to be covered in cash.

Having myself a distaste for either receiving or handing out payment, I decided it would be mutually most comfortable to carry out our commercial transactions as indirectly as possible. The due amount was to be placed in an envelope and left in a small tray in the greenhouse. Any requirements that either of us had were to be noted on a pad hung by the door.

I came to enjoy writing 'Mr J. Jones' on the fibrous brown envelope I had selected as appropriate. Although I checked each day, several weeks passed before I finally received a request – for raffia, 'which I can supply if you wish. Price £2.39.'

He wrote using a gardener's pencil, soft and dark. The letters were each clearly formed and flowing with a regular angularity. I found myself tracing their path.

'Thank you, Mr Jones. Please supply.' Then I added, 'I too prefer raffia.'

He was, as I expected, a most competent and reliable worker. I rarely had to indicate a job that needed attention. Peeling paintwork, loose screws, dripping taps were spotted and remedied without comment. He seemed able to gentle the earth into a soft tilth, easing the path of tender plants so that they flowered earlier and with greater vigour than I remembered. I knew that this was fanciful, but the notion pleased me. I soon began to feel a comfort in his regular comings and goings and in watching him work at each task with quiet persistence.

There was about him an independence of attitude, an assuredness of manner, with nothing of the subservient. He was clearly unimpressed by machines, the aids to my self-sufficiency, acquired on well-meaning advice. I could not resent that, without reference to me, he consigned the expensive motor mower, the strimmer, the leaf blower and shredder to the shed and hauled out equipment and machines long forgotten.

He must have worked on these in his own time, cleaning and sharpening, oiling and setting, until they were fitting companions for his own cherished tools.

I am not such a fool that I did not recognise that I was becoming mesmerised by my enigmatic handyman, but, truthfully, it was not imagination that the cut grass smelt sweeter when mown by a clicking, purring cylinder. There were no more angry sounds of demented disciplining. Mr Jones, Joseph, had brought something of his own silence to my garden.

Of course there were problems.

In the early days, I made an effort to learn the hand shapes of the alphabet, trying to grasp the basics of signing. I hoped to surprise him as I began to combine my fingers and hands to form G...O...O...D ... The effect was as if I had slapped him. Very gently he placed one large hand over mine and held it still, then stepping back, almost in apology, he raised his hand, palm tilted towards me, long, loosely jointed fingers outspread. In exaggerated slow motion, he nodded his head to the right, and gave me the accustomed smile of greeting that he and I both understood.

I recall one particular day. It had been raining – big coins of rain that seemed to kick up the smell of earth. Joseph – I had started to call him Joseph by then – was working in the greenhouse. He loved the build-up of warmth in there and used it almost as a workshop. Although his back was towards me and the door was closed, as clear as the song of the blackbird, I heard whistling, and in the sweet, squeezed notes, I recognised the distinctive pattern of tunes and rhythms from my youth.

The beaker of coffee I had brought for him was almost too hot for my hands, but I cupped it against me, and moving like a predatory cat, sought to prolong the moment and savour the sound. Sweet tendrils of honeysuckle curved over the glass, obscuring the corner, but as I inched onto the shingle surround, the slightest shift of movement was enough to make him aware of my presence.

The whistling stopped. He stood and half turned, as straight as the low angled panes would allow, looked straight at me, gave a broad, all-embracing smile and the exaggerated bow of a performer. The coffee became an accepted tribute and I mimed my applause, and the moment to question had passed.

There was too a misunderstanding over my beloved black elder. Its untrammelled, searching growth had lifted the fragrant pink blossoms beyond my reach, threatening my summer wine production. I wanted him to tidy it, to take the long growth and use the withes as a frame for sweet peas. By chance, I first heard and then saw him lopping through old twisted, varicose branches, exposing the heartwood.

'Stop! Joseph! MISTER Jones, what the hell are you doing?' I knew that I was shrieking.

He spun round, losing his balance on the old apple ladder. The lopper fell forward and he attempted to catch the open blade. Across the pink palm of his hand, a deep gash opened. We watched in horror as crimson blood began to surge from the wound. Instinctively, I tore a towel from the washing line, ripped it into strips and pressed a pad to the flow. His fingers closed over mine increasing the pressure until the flow had been staunched, but not before his blood had seeped between my fingers. Overwhelmed by relief and moved by tenderness, I raised the stains to my lips, and he touched my shoulder, understanding.

I drove to the hospital. The twenty odd miles – penalty of country living – had never threatened to be longer. It was the first time that we had shared so intimate a space and I became intensely aware of his presence. We could each breathe the other, aware of the smoke of a bonfire, smells of cooking and creosote, leather, wax polish and rosemary... skin... hair. Neither of us looked at the other, but the contact, the comfort was palpable.

He wanted to go in alone. There was no doubt of his need for Accident and Emergency treatment, and I had no qualms about his ability to communicate. With the same protective obsession of a mother at the school gate, I watched him walk towards the white doors. Anxious that others should not rush to wrong judgment, I tried to see him with objective eyes, noticing for the first time the slight bandiness of his long legs. A tall man, loose limbed, I liked the suggestion of awareness in the way he inclined his back, or perhaps – I tried to be realistic – it was a stoop of age. If I tried to recapture the first impression I had formed, I would say that he was functionally kempt – his close cropped grey hair, neat like an astrakhan cap. I felt almost proudly possessive as, with his usual gentleness of manner, he stood aside and held the door to aid another patient. For that is what he was – a patient man.

But I am not a patient woman. I tensed to move each time the exit doors slid open, ready to claim him. Unable to sit any longer, I got out of the car at the same time as he came out.

My concentration had been so total that I did not notice the Gaylord sisters approaching. They had grown more like twin walruses than ever – wrapped in shiny black, pendulous bodied, bullet headed and, I swear, with visible moustaches.

'Betty. Betty Preston!' they honked in unison, swaying towards me.

I hurried Joseph towards the car.

'We heard you'd got a man. But nobody told us...' Their beady eyes flashed, exchanging arch looks, jowls wobbling, raising wide nostrils to sniff the air, heads weaving together, apart, in choreographed movement. Then they looked in wonder directly at Joseph and extravagantly mouthed the unspeakable words ...

'HE'S ...BLACK!'

I took Joseph's arm and opened the passenger door, controlling my venom.

'Oh really. How wonderful. I hadn't noticed. And you may be

interested to know that Mr Jones is in fact deaf. But he is not blind.'

I knew that Joseph must have seen their reaction, and I was incensed, furious on his behalf. He felt my anger but did not seem to share it. Instead, he cupped his uninjured hand first across his mouth, then against his eyes and then against an ear and I recognised his mimed philosophy of speak no evil, see no evil, hear no evil. But I knew only too well what pleasure would be taken by those who lived by a more vitriolic code.

Stella's phone call came that evening, even more promptly than I had expected.

'I'm coming to see you.'

Could I possibly guess why? Usually she said, 'I'll come and see you sometime. Or you must come to us, when we are less busy.'

'I'm coming on Thursday morning.'

Surprise, surprise. Any contribution from me was obviously superfluous. My compliance was assumed.

In spite of his injured hand, Joseph was working in the garden when she arrived, tapping vine eyes into the wall, preparing to train the old clematis into better ways. I wished he could have had the same influence on my daughter.

I watched him through the kitchen window while Stella clattered dishes and nosed into cupboards, her high heels irritating on the tiled floor. All the time she was talking, hectoring. It was the brittle tone of exasperation that she assumed to indicate to me, to the world, that she cared.

'I will have my say. You may have forgotten that this was my father's house.'

My home.

'What would he say?'

Very little to me – he never did.

'What about the neighbours?'

What neighbours? Old friends had all moved, were dead, or in care homes. Incomers, weekenders led different lives.

She was generating her own steaming resentment. Her words were such bitter anathema to me that I shut them out, and focused only on what I found pleasing, gentle. I looked at Joseph.

'What do you pay him?'

Not enough, not nearly enough. Her very presence was making me adhere ever more strongly to Joseph. I would pay him more. Ask him to work longer hours...more days.

'And what is all this rubbish about him being deaf?'

I'm listening.

'The Gaylords spoke to Lizzie Frame. Her daughter works in Casualty and she said categorically, CATEGORICALLY, that he spoke just like anyone else. He was able to tell the doctor what happened, AND he heard his name called and could understand everything they said to him.' She chose to emphasise her words by banging a metal spoon on the wooden table, careless of dents, inflicting her damage.

My lack of response was no longer stubborn wilfulness. I was stunned. The pain that flared in my stomach ripped into my heart, and took all breath from my body.

'Now will you get rid of him? He has lied to you.' The final blow.

She and I both recognised her victory.

My eyes could no longer focus. Like my brain, they had become bleary. Joseph had become the prop to my world and he was to be taken away. I was again to be bereft.

I responded with the words and the voice of a stranger.

'I will speak to him. You are right. If he has... misled... me... But not today.'

As Stella perceived me, I felt myself to be – a vulnerable, silly old woman, prey to any self-seeker, victim of my own foolishness.

The next time that Joseph was working in the greenhouse, his territory, concentrating on pricking out seedlings, I stood a little away from the door.

'Mr Jones, please will you come into the house. I wish to speak to you,' and I turned away, steeling myself to composure.

I chose to see him in my sitting room. He was conscious of his working clothes, unwilling to sully the pale colours. My insistence over-rode the awkwardness and he sat. The truth was that, even in my hurt, I could not allow him a cap-in-hand demeanour.

'Why, Joseph? Why should you deceive me?'

Was I expecting shame, explanations, apologies?

He looked at me steadily. And then he spoke: 'When I came to you, we agreed a contract.' His voice was soft, the consonants blurred, the vowels elongated into a rhythm that lulled. He pulled my old postcard once from his pocket.

'These were your terms, and these...' He again simulated a world of silence with his cupped hands... 'were mine.'

I was stunned by the ingenuousness of the man. He forestalled my response.

'I came to you, as I have come to many ladies, to help with odd jobs. This is my contract. What is it that makes these ladies think that because they have paid for my time, they have bought my mind? Mrs Preston, have you any idea of how some of these ladies can talk? Forgive me. Mrs Preston, but a man has to protect himself from the prattling of women.'

I thought of the Gaylords. I thought of Stella in full flow, and I remembered, to my shame, my own strident command. I knew his thoughts matched mine, but there was humour in his eyes, as he said, 'You, my dear Mrs Preston, are not a prattling woman.'

I took the postcard from him, picked up a soft pencil, 3B as I remember, and added: 'Good Sense of Humour absolutely essential. Must be able to whistle 'Stardust'.

So Joseph stayed, splashing my muted garden with the vibrance of Canna lilies, and we drank the elderflower wine, and my world felt good again, listening to the garden, and speaking volumes.

My, how that man can talk!

THE BOWER BIRD

by **Ann Kelley**

Luath Press Ltd

THE BOWER BIRD

by **Ann Kelley**

Gussie lives in Cornwall and, like most twelve year olds, is quickly growing up. She is also awaiting news of a heart transplant operation. When Gussie moves from the coast to a new house in town, she rebels, discovers her ancestors and an interest in photography, falls in love and has parent troubles – all whilst experiencing general adolescent angst and trying not to wait for what might never happen.

Ann Kelley *is a photographer and prize-winning poet. She has previously published a collection of poems and photographs, a book of photos of St Ives families and an audio book of cat stories. She lives with her second husband and several cats in Cornwall.*

"The world of life and death, beauty and truth seen through the eyes of a 12 year old girl. A rare and beautiful book of lasting quality – we felt this is a voice that needs to be heard and read."

Judges
David Almond – Author
Marilyn Brocklehurst – Proprietor, Norfolk Children's Book Centre
Julia Somerville – Broadcaster and journalist
Isha Amin (Young Judge) – First News competition winner
Amar Mann (Young Judge) – First News competition winner

THE BOWER BIRD

For my wonderful family

ONE

WE'VE BEEN HERE for two weeks. I'm still not well enough to start at the local school. But the weather has been barmy – or is it balmy? Yes, it probably is balmy. Barmy means daft. The sun has shone on us most days since we moved, and I feel that my heart is going to mend enough to have the operation that could give me a few more years of life.

It's a cold night and the sky is clear. Stars are appearing one by one. I wear my distance specs to see them otherwise it's all a beautiful blur. I sit in my window on a stripy cushion and feel... happy.

The lights of the little town are twinkling below me, and there is a nearly full moon – its blue-white wedding veil draped across the bay. The lighthouse winks its bright eye every ten seconds.

I did have a bedside lamp on but moths kept coming in the window to commit suicide. Why do insects that choose to fly around in total darkness have a fatal attraction for hot light bulbs? They must be barmy. Or maybe a hot bulb gives off a smell like female moths and the male moths are attracted to it for that reason.

Even in the middle of the night seagulls are flying all around us, calling to each other in the dark. The wind has got up and the gulls are lifting on invisible currents and then swoop fast like shooting stars.

Our young gull is crouched on the ridge of the roof, his head poking out over the top, watching the adults and whining pathetically. There must be some juvenile gulls up there learning how to fly and land cleanly on the rooftops and chimneys, just as if they are alighting on cliff ledges.

I scrunch up under a warm woolly blanket with my feet up,

and Charlie keeps trying to get comfortable but there's no horizontal bit. She prefers me to be flat in bed so she can warm herself on my tummy, or my chest. She shouldn't really sit on my chest as I have trouble breathing at the best of times and anyway, I had open-heart surgery last year, when I was eleven, and the healing process hasn't finished yet. The operation was a waste of time. It was supposed to be one of three procedures to repair the various heart defects. When I was opened up they could see that I had no pulmonary artery, not even an excuse for one, and there was nothing to build on. So the surgeon just closed me up again I now have an amazing scar that cuts me in half almost, as if I have survived a shark attack.

Poor Charlie, she doesn't understand why I don't want her on my chest.

I reluctantly leave the starlit night and get into my bed. I'm reading a really good book by Mary Webb called *Gone to Earth*. It's about a girl who has a pet fox. Mary Webb has written several other books. I'll have to look out for them at car boot sales or in the second-hand bookshop, as they are so old they are probably out of print.

As usual, the three cats wake me. Charlie is the noisiest and the most demanding. As soon as there's a glimmer of daylight she starts on at me to get up and feed her. She meows loudly and jumps on the bed and marches up and down on one spot, as if I am her mother and she is trying to make the milk come. She sounds quite cross. If I pretend to sleep she gets really irate. The other two are more patient but they stare, accusingly. I can feel their eyes on me. Flo sits on the chest of drawers and Rambo on the window seat.

I wake to a completely pink dawn. Outside everything is saturated with an intense rosy glow. Pink sky, sea and bay. Pink roofs, candy sand. I yearned for a party dress when I was five or six, of exactly this shade – to match my Barbie doll's outfit.

By the time I find my specs, put on a dressing gown and flip-flops, load a film into my camera and lean out the window, the pink has paled and silvered, but the sun now hangs heavily above the dunes, like a red balloon full of liquid. One small boat chugs out of the harbour dragging a pink wake and gulls are following in a raucous rush.

I am surrounded by hungry cats. I better give in. Charlie is jubilant, running ahead down the stairs, calling me to hurry up. The others follow behind me.

I have to go to the bathroom first, and this really makes Charlie cross. She never knows whether to come in with me at this point, because she usually spends bath-time with me, but now she can only think about her rumbling stomach.

Mum is in the bathroom for longer and longer every morning. What does she do in there? She told me once that she hadn't had a decent crap since I was born. First I screamed all the time, then as I got bigger I banged on the door and yelled. When I was a baby I screamed for twenty-one hours once – she wasn't in the bathroom all that time, of course. She says I'm lucky to be alive as she nearly strangled me several times. Sleep deprivation makes you go barmy apparently.

'Mum, I have to wee, I'm desperate.'

She's looking into a magnifying mirror and doing something disgusting with scissors up her nose.

'Ohmygod, Mum, that's gross. You'll slice through your mucus membranes.'

'They're blunt-ended, Gussie. You wait until you get hairy nostrils. See how you like it.'

Hopefully I won't live that long.

She does all this other stuff, too, to her face, plucking and scraping and applying various very expensive unguents. What a lovely word – unguents.

'Is it worth it, Mum?'

'Probably not, but I'm not giving up just yet.'

She's actually quite cool looking, I think, but because she had me when she was forty-one she is quite old now. It doesn't bother me much, but it bothers her. She's shaving her armpits now. What a palaver. I don't have any pubic hair yet, as I am small for my age – my heart wants me to be small, so it doesn't have to work too hard.

'Mum, can I help unpack something today?'

'Yeah, why not? We'll have a look in some of the smaller boxes from Grandma's.'

Grandma was small and plump and she knitted and sewed, tatted, smocked and embroidered. You never saw her without something in her hands that she was working on. Their garden was a fruit bowl of gooseberries and blackcurrants, redcurrants and raspberries, loganberries and strawberries. I used to throw a tennis ball up onto the roof of their bungalow and catch it when it bounced off the gutter. Another game with the ball was to roll it along the wavy low brick wall, which went around the front garden, and see how far it would go before it fell off. I got quite good at that.

They lived in Shoeburyness, quite close to London, where we lived when we were still a family, before Daddy left.

Like me, he's an only child. His parents, who I never met, came from this town.

Mum doesn't have any brothers or sisters either, so I have no aunts, uncles or cousins on her side of the family. There's only Mum now. Except that we are called Stevens and there are at least a hundred Stevenses in St Ives. I am determined to find my lost Cornish family, somehow.

Daddy isn't being at all helpful. He keeps saying he'll let me have his family tree, but he hasn't even given me a leaf yet. Mum is being positively obstructive: she doesn't want anything to do with Daddy's family and assumes they won't want anything to do with us. Anything Daddy related is a no-no. She has the screaming abdabs if I even mention him.

There's a wildlife warden we met out at Peregrine Cottage – the house we rented on the cliff – who said she has some relations called Stevens, but I've sort of lost touch with her since we moved. Ginnie.

It's sad how people drift in and out of our lives. Like my London friend Summer. I call her my friend, but I haven't seen her since we came to Cornwall. Maybe now we're settled in our own house, she will come and stay during school holidays. Or maybe

I'll never see her again.

I don't suppose I'll ever see Shoeburyness again. Or smell the smell of it: cockle shells and seaweed and mud. The tide comes in very fast from a long way out, where the longest pier in the world ends. The water is a muddy brow colour though, not like the clear blue-green of St Ives. But there were wooden breakwaters to climb and balance on and I liked the pebbly beach, and finding white quartz stones to rub together to make a spark. Illuminations and neon lights shone all along the Golden Mile at Southend, where we bought fish and chips. Under the arches of a bridge there's a row of cafés with striped awnings and plastic tables and chairs set out on the pavement. Cafés with nautical names like The Mermaid, The Barge, Captain's Table. That was where I had my first experiences of eating out: sausage and mash or egg and chips, always with a cup of tea.

Grandpop and Grandma would take me to the pebbly beach and they'd hire deckchairs and we'd have fish-paste sandwiches and apples for tea. I could still run and climb then, and I would jump from roof to roof of the beach huts. (The beach huts had names too: *Sunny Days, Happy Days, Cosy Corner, Chez Nous.* That's French for *Our House.*)

Grandma was scandalised and tried to stop me, but Grandpop would cheer me on.

'You can do it princess.'

I don't look like a princess. I am small for my age and skinny and my skin is rather mauvish, I think. My hair Mum calls dark blonde, but to be honest it's mouse. 'Nothing Wrong with Mouse.'

'Oh, the elephants!' I unpack a troupe of elephants, three of them, each one a bit bigger than the one before, all with turned up ivory tusks and mother of pearl toes. I remember them standing on a window ledge. They are made of some heavy black wood, and carved. Looking closely, I see that they are slightly damaged – a piece of ear gone here, a tusk there. I remember them as being perfect, and Grandma saying, 'Be careful, my love.' I used to invent journeys for them across Africa, searching for greener pastures. I imagined them as a family – father, mother and baby. The mother has to do that on her own.

There's a pink-brown stone Buddha too, which I always loved to hold as it felt cold even on the hottest day, as if it contained something otherworldly. It has a smiling face, as if this god has a sense of humour. You don't get that impression about Jesus or God.

'Where shall we put them, Mum?'

'Have them in your room if you want.'

I put them on the stairs so I can carry them up next time I climb to my attic room. There are little piles of towels and sheets, clothes and books there already, waiting to be carried to their homes, like travellers in family groups at a bus station.

Grandpop travelled all over the world when he was in the Royal Navy and brought back lots of exotic souvenirs. We unpack a Japanese tea set they used to keep safe in a glass cabinet, thin porcelain coloured red and gold with little figures and landscapes.

'We'll use these,' Mum says.

'But aren't they terribly precious and worth lots of money?'

'No, it's only Japanese export stuff. We should enjoy them. What's the point of having pretty things gathering dust?'

Mum's good about stuff like that. She never makes a fuss if I break something. They're Only Things and Accidents Happen. I pick up a cup and look through it at the sun shining. It's a lovely thing.

'No dishwasher for these, Gussie, you'll have to wash them by hand.'

'No probs, Mum.' I am learning how to speak Strine – Australian – for when and if my new friend Brett comes to see me. No Worries. Crikey.

Mum sleeps in the main bedroom, the master bedroom, or I suppose it should be called the mistress bedroom, on the floor below me. There's a big bay window and the same view that I have, but slightly lower of course. The terrace faces south, there's plenty of sunshine all day long, and there's a little slab of concrete along the front path that gets the last of the sun. We sit there together on cushions and she drinks her whisky and I have a freshly squeezed orange juice or elderflower juice and we talk.

I think we talk more easily because we are not looking at each other. It's as if we are in a car, sitting next to each other, but looking ahead, and it's easier to say important things if you are not looking into each other's eyes. We have our eyes closed, because the sun is still so bright, and it's as if we are in a dream. I feel close to Mum when we talk like that.

'Don't you still love Daddy just a little bit? 'I sometimes ask.

'No I bloody don't. He slept with other women. Why should I love him?'

'Okay, okay. I only asked.'

'I still feel very hurt, Gussie. Bastard! He betrayed me – us. He betrayed us.'

'Yeah, but if he wanted you to forgive him and he wanted to be with us, here, now, what would you say?'

'Fuck off, probably.' She sniffs. 'Anyway,, we're okay on our own, aren't we?'

'I suppose.'

CHAPTER TWO

MUM HAS GONE out for the evening with Dr Dobbs – Alistair.

I'm playing Scrabble with Mrs Lorn. She is letting me win without much of a fight. Also I keep getting good letters – the high scoring C, Q and X so far. I put down all my letters straight away – QUIXOTIC, how about that! That's got to be the best score I've ever had. Probably the best score anyone has ever had in the entire history of Scrabble – 72, as it was on a double word score, plus 50 for putting down all my letters at once. She's getting all the rubbish, lots of vowels. She calls me 'my girl' with an extra 'r' in girl. Mrs Lorn has this habit of whistling when she's thinking – hymns, mostly. Sometimes she breaks into song. I do like Scrabble. I wish I wasn't winning so easily though. She's so old, she has probably given up the idea of winning.

'How old are you, Mrs Lorn?'

'As old as my feet but younger than my teeth and hair.'

She cackles like an old witch. 'Anyway, my girl, don't you know it's bad manners to ask a lady her age?'

'Why is it? Mum says she's fifty-two but her tits are only thirty-nine.'

Mrs Lorn screams with shocked laughter.

I like old people, apart from when they hug me or do that thing with my lips, you know, pinch them together so your mouth is an O and they make you say 'Sausages'. Though no one's done that to me for years. It's a torture aimed solely at small children who can't defend themselves. Like when they pull off your nose and show it to you and put it back again before you realise it's only their thumb and your nose is still where it always was, in the middle of your face. You've got to be very young to believe that. When you get to five it's too late, except for Father Christmas and fairies.

When I was three I can remember sitting at the window on Christmas Eve and I saw Father Christmas's sleigh pulled by reindeer in the sky. I really believed I saw it.

It must be wonderful to grow old like Mrs Lorn and know so much and have experienced a lot of life. It must make you wise if you can remember all those things you have heard and seen and read.

There's an old man who has three retriever dogs on leads accompanying him as he braves the roads at Carbis Bay in his electric wheelchair. He looks very heroic, as if he's in a horse-drawn chariot or on a dog sledge. I haven't seen him for a while, not since we left the cottage. We used to wave to him from the car but he didn't wave back. Probably he isn't able to. I wonder what he knows, and what he used to do before he became lopsided? And another very old man, always dressed immaculately in tweed suit and pork pie hat, straw hat in summer (Mr Dapper we call him), walks with the help of a stick all the way from Carbis Bay to St Ives and back each morning along the main road. He looks sad. Lonely. He's a guest at an old people's home.

Why do they put old people's homes in out of the way places? If I were old I would want to be in the middle of things, not on the outside ready to be shoved out of life when the time came. I suppose that's what I felt like when I was in the wilderness out at the cottage on the cliff. Apart from society. An outcast, cast away. Here in St Ives there's human life all around me.

Mum and Alistair have come back and he's off again, giving Mrs Lorn a lift home. She was delighted.

Mum looks flushed and smells of cigarettes and whisky and other people's beer. Her hair looks good. Her skirt's a bit short though. She must like him a lot.

Alistair's not half as handsome as Daddy. Daddy looks like a cross between Keanu Reeves and Bob Geldof, but not as scruffy as Bob Geldof. Alistair looks like a Dobbin horse, with his big ears and long face and nose. But he has kind eyes and a nice smile and always wears interesting ties. It must be difficult being a man and having to wear boring suits to work. I suppose a tie is one item you can decorate yourself with.

Like the bower bird. I think they attract females by making their nests, or bowers, look interesting.

'Bed, Gussie, Bed. Off You Go, Late. Late. Late.'

'Where did you go, Mum? Did you have a good time?'

'Sloop Inn. Fun, it was fun.'

'Did you meet anyone?'

'Alistair knows everyone.'

'Might he know Dad's relations, do you think?'

'Gussie. It's not the sort of thing you ask a man the first time he takes you out. You ask him. I'm going to bed, and You Should Too. Tired. You Look Tired.'

'Okay, okay, I'm going.'

I take my time getting upstairs, stop halfway to stroke Flo, who is on guard on the landing. She is such a school prefect, always keeping the other two cats in order, on their toes. I would be too, in their shoes... interesting, these foot metaphors or whatever. Standing up for your beliefs. Filling his shoes. Knocking the socks off... Language is interesting.

I'd like to go to a school where they teach Latin, so I could study the roots of words. The local school is good apparently, but doesn't have Latin. I'll have to teach myself if I really want to learn. There was a *Winnie the Pooh* in Latin at our last house. *Winnie ille Pu.*

Lucus Lucubris Joris is Eeyore's Gloomy Place, which is *tristis et palustris*, rather boggy and sad.

Locus inondatus – floody place.

Domus mea – my house.

What about this one! *Fovea insidiosa ad heffalumpus catandos idonea* (Pooh trap for heffalumps).

I wrote those down so I could remember them. They were on the maps at both ends of the book. I like maps. There are lovely maps on the end pages of the Swallows and Amazons books too.

Mum said she entered her O-level German oral exam only knowing two phrases. One of them was – *Ich erkannte ihn an seinem Bart* – I recognised him by his beard. And the other phrase was – *Ich muss nach Hause gehen* – I must go home now. She managed to incorporate both into her conversation, and charmed the examiner with her knowledge of art – there was a Pieter Brueghel print to talk about. She spoke English for most of the time and still passed.

I don't believe everything she tells me. She's a dreadful exaggerator.

Mum potters about downstairs, filling the dishwasher and putting the washing in the drier. Then she comes up too, carrying her hot water bottle. She feels the cold almost as much as me.

It's comforting having her in the room below, moving about, snoring in her sleep.

Our gulls are settled on the roof, hunkered down for the night, their heads tucked under their wings. There's no moon tonight and it's very cloudy. The wind is coming from the back of the house, the west, so I can open the front window without it rattling.

Tomorrow I'll go to the library and look for poetry books. There were loads at our last place.

I wonder if I'll ever meet Mr Writer – that's my name for the man who owns Peregrine Cottage. Maybe he's a murderer doing time. Or a famous poet on a world tour. He could be a bank manager, or a drug dealer, or a gunrunner. So many possibilities. Does anyone ever want to grow up to be a gunrunner or a car park attendant or a dinner lady?

I always wanted to be a cowboy until I realised, because I was a girl I could never ever be a cow*boy*. I was devastated that God had done this to me. It wasn't fair.

It didn't stop me dressing as a boy for quite a while afterwards though. I felt I had to gradually dissolve my boyhood and think myself slowly into being a girl. It wasn't easy.

I find it hard to go to sleep sometimes. I feel it's a waste of time, sleeping, when I could be reading or living. But then, dreaming is a sort of living, I suppose. I often have an exciting time in my dreams, more so than in my ordinary life. Sometimes in the middle of a dream one of the cats wakes me (chasing and killing something usually) and I get frustrated by the interruption. I usually forget an interrupted dream. Why is it so difficult to remember dreams? I feel cheated if I can't remember what happened.

Last night there were two birds. One was a little white owl sitting quietly on top of the book shelf in my room. The other was a miniature rail, buff and apricot coloured with black sharp beak, black legs and wide spread long black toes. It became scarlet and emerald, and stepped carefully across my books, as if they were water lily leaves. I think there is a bird called a Jesus bird – because it looks like it's walking on water. It might have been one of those.

My own room: I do like it. All my babyhood is on the top shelf of the large book case: faded and worn Teddy, who has never had another name; Panda, from a trip Daddy made to Germany; Nightie Dog, that used to be Mum's and has a zip in its tummy for pyjamas; several knitted toys, including Noddy, that Grandma made for me. He's very old and his colours have faded but his bell still rings on the end of his night cap. And Rena Wooflie, my favourite, a soft stuffed girl dog with checked dress and apron. Mum bought her for me in Mombasa the very first time we went to Africa, because I had lost my cuddly comfort blanket on the journey.

I love Rena Wooflie and she has to come with me to hospital. It's for her sake, not mine. She gets lonely, as she doesn't talk the same language as Panda or Teddy or Nightie Dog. Rena Wooflie and I speak Swahili together.

jambo – hello
abari? – how are you?
msuri – good
paka – cat
malaika – angel
kuku – fowl
simba – lion
nyuki – bee
kidege – a little bird
kufa tutakufa wote – as for dying, we shall all die.

That's all I know really but I do still have a phrase book so I could in theory learn some more.

That first winter in Africa there was a family with a little boy about my age – three – and he was desperate for my Rena Wooflie. No matter that he had hundreds of teddies and soft toys, he wanted my one and only. My mum bought another one and gave it to him. Its head wasn't quite the same angle as my Rena Wooflie's and he started to moan and grizzle, and he threw it and yelled, and his mother picked it up and yanked its head around and said – Is that better? And I could tell she was pretending it was her little boy's head she was twisting, not the toy's.

I would never abuse my Rena Wooflie.

On top of my wardrobe, looking down at me is Horsey. He was my baby walker, a horse on wheels. Mum tried to throw him away once because the metal neck pole had pushed through the straw and fur and his head was in danger of coming off. She placed Horsey by the dustbins the day before dustbin day, and then it started to rain so she brought him in again. That was years ago. He's still here, mended of course with a new patch of different coloured fake fur. He's part of the family now.

Noah's Ark completes childhood on the high shelf. It was Mum's when she was little. There are pairs of little wooden hand-painted lions and elephants, sheep and cows, hippos and zebra, and I've added other tiny animals found over the years – a lead crocodile, a glass cat, a wooden cat, and my favourite, a giraffe made of bone.

WHAT WAS LOST

by **Catherine O'Flynn**

Tindal
Street
Press

WHAT WAS LOST

by **Catherine O'Flynn**

A lost little girl with her notebook and toy monkey appears on the CCTV screens of the Green Oaks shopping centre, evoking memories of junior detective, Kate Meaney, missing for 20 years. Kurt, a security guard with a sleep disorder and Lisa, a disenchanted deputy manager at Your Music, follow her through the centre's endless corridors – welcome relief from customers, colleagues and the Green Oaks mystery shopper. But, as this after-hours friendship grows in intensity, it brings new loss and new longing to light.

Catherine O'Flynn *was born in Birmingham in 1970, where she grew up in and around her parents' sweet shop. She has worked as a teacher, a web editor, a mystery customer and a postwoman – and her first novel draws on her experience of working in record stores. After a few years in Barcelona, she now lives in Birmingham.*

"A formidable novel blending humour and pathos in a cleverly constructed and absorbing mystery. An extraordinary book and a superb first novel."

Judges
Nic Bottomley – General Manager of Mr B's Emporium of Reading Delights
Helen Lederer – Actress and writer
Sebastian Shakespeare – Evening Standard columnist and diary editor

WHAT WAS LOST

Written for Peter, and dedicated to the memory of
Donal of Hillstreet and Ellen of Oylegate

1

Crime was out there. Undetected, unseen. She hoped she wouldn't be too late. The bus driver was keeping the bus at a steady 15 m.p.h., braking at every approaching green light until it turned red. She closed her eyes and continued the journey in her head as slowly as she could. She opened them, but still the bus lagged far behind her worst projection. Pedestrians overtook them, the driver whistled.

She looked at the other passengers and tried to deduce their activities for the day. Most were pensioners and she counted four instances of the same huge, blue checked shopping bag. She made a note of the occurrence in her pad; she knew better than to believe in coincidences.

She read the adverts on the bus. Most were adverts for adverts: 'If you're reading this, then so could your customers.' She wondered if any of the passengers ever took out advertising space on the bus, and what they would advertise if they did.

'Come and enjoy my big, blue, checked shopping bag, it is filled with catfood'

'I will talk to anyone about anything. I also eat biscuits.'

'Mr and Mrs Roberts, officially recognized brewers of the world's strongest tea. "We squeeze the bag."

'I smell strange, but not unpleasantly.'

Kate thought she would like to take out an advert for the agency. The image would be a silhouette of her and Mickey within the lens of a magnifying glass. Below, it would say:

She made another note in her pad of the phone number on the advert, to be rung at some later date when the office was fully operational.

Eventually the bus reached the landscaped lawns and forlorn, fluttering flags of the light industrial estates that surrounded the newly opened Green Oaks Shopping Centre. She paid particular attention to unit 15 on the Langsdale Estate, where she had once witnessed what seemed to be an argument between two men. One man had a large moustache, the other wore sunglasses and no jacket on what had been a cold day – she'd thought they both looked of criminal character. After some deliberation and subsequent sightings of a large white van outside the unit, she had come to the conclusion that the two men were trafficking diamonds. Today all was quiet at the unit.

She opened her pad at a page with 'Unit 15 Surveillance' written at the top. Next to that day's date she wrote in the slightly jerky bus writing that dominated the page: 'No sighting. Collecting another shipment from Holland?'

Fifteen minutes later Kate was walking through the processed air of the Market Place of Green Oaks. Market Place wasn't a market place. It was the subterranean part of the shopping centre, next to the bus terminals, reserved for the non-prestige, low-end stores: fancy goods stores, cheap chemists, fake perfume sellers, stinking butchers, flammable-clothes vendors. Their smells mingled with the smell of burnt dust from the over-door heaters and made her feel sick. This was as far as most of Kate's fellow passengers ventured into the centre. It was the closest approximation of the tatty old High Street, which had suffered a rapid decline since the centre had opened. Now when the bus drove up the High Street no one liked to look at the reproachful boarded-up doorways filled with fast-food debris and leaves.

She realized that it was Wednesday and that she'd forgotten to buy that week's copy of the *Beano* from her usual newsagent. She had no choice but to go to the dingy kiosk in the centre to get it. Afterwards she stood and looked again at the *True Detective* magazines on the shelf. The woman on the front didn't look like a detective. She was wearing a trilby and raincoat…but nothing else. She looked like someone from a *Two Ronnies* sketch. Kate didn't like it.

She rode the escalator up to the ground floor, where the proper shops, the fountains and plastic palms began. It was the school holidays, but too early to be busy. None of her classmates was allowed to go to the centre without their parents. Sometimes she'd bump into a family group with one of her peers in tow and would exchange awkward greetings. She had picked up a sense that adults tended to be uncomfortable with her solo trips out and about, so now whenever questioned by shop assistant, security guard or parent she would always imply that an unspecified adult relative was just off in another store. Largely, though, no one questioned her, in fact no one ever really seemed to see her at all. Sometimes Kate thought she was invisible.

It was 9.30 a.m. She retrieved her laboriously type-written agenda from her back pocket:

09.30-10.45	Tandy: research walkie talkies and microphones
10.45-12.00	general centre surveillance
12.00-12.45	lunch at Vanezi's
12.45-13.30	Midland Educational: look at ink pads for fingerprinting
13.30-15.30	surveillance by banks
15.30	bus home

Kate hurried on to Tandy.

*

She was flustered to arrive at Vanezi's restaurant a good twenty minutes past noon. This was not the way a professional operated. This was sloppy. She waited by the door to be seated, though she could see her table was still free. The same lady as usual took her to the same table as usual and Kate slid into the orange plastic booth which offered a view out over the main atrium of the centre.

'Do you need to see the menu today?' asked the waitress.

'No thanks. Can I have the Children's Special please with a banana float? And can I not have any cucumber on the beefburger, please?'

'It's not cucumber, it's gherkin, love.'

Kate made a note of this in her pad: 'Gherkins/cucumbers – not same thing: research difference.' She'd hate to blow her cover on a Stateside mission with a stupid error like that.

Kate looked at the big plastic tomato-shaped tomato-sauce dispenser on her table. They were one of her favourite things – they made total sense.

At school last term, Paul Roberts had read out his essay, 'The best birthday ever', which culminated in his grandparents and parents taking him out to Vanezi's for dinner. He spoke of eating spaghetti with meatballs, which for some reason he and everyone else in the class had found funny. He was still excited as he rushed through his story of drinking ice-cream floats and ordering a Knickerbocker Glory. He said it was brilliant.

Kate couldn't understand why he didn't just take himself there on a Saturday lunchtime if he liked it so much. She could even take him the first time and tell him the best place to sit. She could show him the little panel on the wall that you could slide back to reveal all the dirty plates passing by on a conveyor belt. She could tell him how one day she hoped to place some kind of auto-shutter action camera on the belt, which could travel around the entire restaurant taking surveillance shots unseen, before returning to Kate. She could point out the washing-up man who she thought might be murderous, and perhaps Paul could help her stake him out. She could maybe invite him to join the agency (if Mickey approved).

But she didn't say anything. She just wondered.

She glanced around to check that no one could see, then she reached into her bag and pulled out Mickey. She sat him next to her by the window, so that the waitress wouldn't notice, and where he had a good view of the people below. She was training Mickey up to be her partner in the agency. Generally Mickey just did surveillance work. He was small enough to be unobtrusive despite his rather outlandish get-up. Kate liked Mickey's outfit even though it meant he didn't blend in as well as he might. He wore a pin-striped gangster suit with spats. The spats slightly spoiled the Sam Spade effect, but Kate liked them anyway; in fact she wanted a pair herself.

Mickey had been made from a craft kit called 'Sew your own Charlie Chimp the Gangster' given to Kate by an auntie. Charlie had languished along with all of Kate's other soft toys throughout most of her childhood, but when she'd started up the detective agency last year she thought he looked the part. Charlie Chimp was no good though. Instead he became Mickey the Monkey. Kate would run through their agenda with him each morning and he always travelled with her in the canvas army surplus bag.

The waitress brought the order. Kate ate the burger and perused the first Beano of the new year, while Mickey kept a steady eye on some suspicious teenagers below.

2

Kate lived a bus journey away from Green Oaks. Her home was in the only Victorian block of houses left in the area, a red-brick three-storey outcrop which looked uncomfortable amidst the grey and white council-built cuboids. Kate's house was sandwiched between a newsagent's shop on one side, and a butcher and greengrocer on the other. Her house had clearly also been a shop once, but now a net curtain hung across the front window and what had been the shop was a sitting room where Kate's grandmother spent her long afternoons watching quiz shows.

The house was the only one in the block not to function as a business (aside from Kate's putative agency operation), and it was also the only one used as a home. None of her shopkeeper neighbours lived above their shops; at around six o'clock each evening they would shut up and depart for their semis in the suburbs, leaving silence and emptiness on all sides of Kate's room.

Kate knew and liked the shopkeepers well. The greengrocer's was run by Eric and his wife Mavis. They had no children, but they were always kind to Kate and bought her a surprisingly well-judged Christmas present each year. Last year it had been a Spirograph, which Kate had used to make a professional-looking logo on her business cards. Now her time was taken up with the agency and constant surveillance activity, Kate had less time to visit the couple, but still once a week she would pop in for a cup of tea and, swinging her legs from the stool behind the counter, she would listen to Radio 2 and watch the customers buy vast quantities of potatoes.

Next to Eric and Mavis was Mr Watkin the butcher. Mr Watkin was an old man, Kate estimated probably seventy-eight. He was a nice man with a nice wife, but very few people bought their meat from him any more. Kate thought this possibly had something to do with the way Mr Watkin stood in his shop window swatting flies against the sides of meat with a large palette knife. It was also perhaps a self-perpetuating situation, in that the fewer customers Mr Watkin had, the less meat he stocked, and the less meat he had, the less he looked like a butcher, and the more he looked like a crazy old man who collected and displayed bits of flesh in his front window. The previous week Kate had passed the window to see it contained only a single rabbit (and Kate was sure the only person alive who still ate rabbit was in fact Mr Watkin himself), some kidneys, a chicken, a side of pork and a string of sausages. This in itself was nothing too remarkable for Mr Watkin, but what caused Kate to stop and stare was an apparent new marketing initiative by the butcher. Evidently he had become a little embarrassed by the minimal nature of his window displays and so perhaps in order to make them seem less odd (and this is where Kate felt he'd really miscalculated), he had arranged the items in a jaunty tableau. Thus it appeared that the chicken was taking the rabbit for a walk by its lead of sausages, over a hillock of pork under a dark red kidney sun. Kate looked up from the grisly scene to see Mr Watkin nodding at her in amazement from inside the shop, thumbs aloft, as if taken aback by his own flair.

On the other side of Kate's house was Mr Palmer the newsagent. Mr Palmer worked alongside his son Adrian, who was the closest Kate had to a best friend, and was also the first and so far only client of Falcon Investigations. Adrian was twenty-two and had been to university. Mr Palmer had wanted Adrian to get a 'proper career' after graduation, but Adrian had no such ambitions, and was happy to spend his days reading behind the counter and helping to run the small business. The Palmer family lived in a modern semi on the outskirts of town, but the mother and sister rarely visited the shop – sweet-selling was left to the men of the family. Adrian treated Kate like an adult, but then Adrian treated everyone the same. He wasn't capable of putting on a different face for different customers as his father did. Mr Palmer could switch from an avuncular 'Now then, young man', to an utterly sincere 'Such a shocking headline, isn't it, Mrs Stevens?' in seconds.

But, whatever Adrian's enthusiasms were, he tended to assume they were shared by all, or at least would be if he spread the word. He spent his afternoons buried in the NME or reading books about musicians. He would earnestly recommend albums to his customers, seemingly blind to the improbability of Mrs Docherty suddenly switching from Foster and Allen to the MC5, or Debbie Casey and her giggling teenage pals ever finding much of significance in Leonard Cohen. As soon as Mr Palmer left him alone in the shop, Jimmy Young's radio show would be switched off and Adrian would slip a tape into the tinny radio cassette player. He thought that the reason no one ever asked him what was playing was because they were a little shy, so he would always put a scrawled sign on the counter: 'Now playing: Captain Beefheart, *Lick My Decals Off, Baby*. For more information just ask a member of staff'.

With Kate, though, Adrian liked to talk about crime detection, about classic detective movies, about which customers might be killers, about where they might have hidden their victims' bodies. Adrian would always come up with the most inventive body dumps. Sometimes Kate would go with Adrian to the wholesalers, advising him on what sweets to buy, and they would look at the burly warehousemen and assess which of them had criminal records.

Adrian knew about Falcon Investigations, though not about Mickey. Mickey was top secret. Mr Palmer had been getting increasingly irate about schoolkid sweet pilfering and so Adrian contracted Falcon Investigations to carry out a security assessment of the store. Kate told him that her rate was £1 a day plus expenses. She said she expected the assessment to take half a day at the most and no expenses would be incurred as she lived next door, and so she prepared an invoice for 50p. Kate was indescribably elated at this 'proper' commission. She even went out and bought a real invoice pad with duplicate sheets, which at 75p put the P & L in deficit, but she was building for the future. Kate asked Adrian to act as he normally would do when working in the shop and she played the part of a shoplifter. She said this was essential for her to pinpoint weak spots. After twenty minutes Kate left the shop and returned to the office to write up the report. She presented it to Adrian a couple of hours later, along with 37p worth of sweets she had managed to lift. The report was in two parts, the first detailing her time in the shop, the second making recommendations to 'stamp out crime'. These involved a rearrangement of some of the loose pocket-money sweets, a complete overhaul of the crisp display rack and the positioning of two mirrors at strategic points.

Adrian treated the report with the seriousness in which it had been compiled and carried out the recommendations to the letter. Mr Palmer was delighted with the results and pilfering was brought to a virtual standstill. Kate asked Mr Palmer if he would write down any positive comments he had about the service, as she had seen other businesses use such personal testimonials on promotional material. She imagined her advert on the bus garlanded with sincere plaudits:

'*We received a rapid, professional service at very reasonable rates.*'
'*Our agent was confidential, tactful and most of all EFFECTIVE.*'
'*Crime rates have plummeted since we called in Falcon Investigations.*'

She was then slightly disappointed to receive instead from Mr Palmer: 'Good girl, Kate! You're a little treasure!!'

3

Each time she visited Green Oaks, Kate always paid a visit to Midland Educational, the large stationery store. Today's ostensible reason had been to examine their range of ink pads, but Kate always found some excuse to spend time in the store. Hours flew by.

Although Sam Spade is not seen at any point during *The Maltese Falcon* shopping for stationery, Kate knew how important premium office supplies were to an effective investigator. In fact stationery was something of a growing problem for Kate. At the start of last term, she had been taken for the first time into the stationery cupboard at school. Mrs Finnegan told Kate that she would be Stationery Monitor and gave her a thorough run-through of her forthcoming duties and responsibilities. She was puzzled as to why the always attentive Kate seemed lost in a world of her own.

Mrs Finnegan: It is vital that for every new exercise book given out you must collect the signed corner snipping from the old, filled exercise book. These must be collected in this Tupperware container and at the end of the week the number in the container must correspond exactly with the decrease in the number of exercise books you record in the Audit Register. Does that all make sense, Kate?

Kate: …

Mrs Finnegan: Kate?

Kate had not been prepared for the level of riches in the stationery cupboard. First, it was not a cupboard, it was a room.

Secondly, it was evident that the full range of stationery she and her classmates had ever used were but tiny and very dull drops in the vast ocean of the cupboard. The room contained luxury items like multi-coloured Biros, metal pencil sharpeners, entire packets of felt-tips alongside serious, high-end items like concertina files and jumbo staplers. Kate didn't hear a word Mrs Finnegan said because she was in a state of actual, physical shock.

Since that afternoon the cupboard had played on her mind. She knew it was important for an investigator to get inside the criminal mind, but she suspected the motives of her brain's endless inventiveness in how to run rings around the audit register. She feared she was being pulled towards corruption.

Today in Midland Educational she had spent thirty minutes looking at ink stamps, trying to think of a reason for needing one but failing. Now Kate was doing her usual stint outside the banks and building societies. She had been watching them for over an hour. Two banks and three building societies were all situated next to each other on level 2 of the centre next to the children's play area. Between them was an oasis of imitation plant life surrounded by orange plastic seats. Kate sat with Mickey poking discreetly out of the bag by her side.

She had always thought if any significant crime was going to happen at the centre it would have to be here. She was sure of it. The security guards were all too busy watching shoplifters and truants, but Kate had her eye on the big picture and one day the hours she put in would pay off. Sometimes she allowed herself to think about the kind of civic reception she'd get when she foiled her first major robbery. In the *Beano*, good deeds were rewarded with a 'slap-up meal' invariably consisting of a mountain of mashed potato with sausages poking out. Kate hoped for something more like a medal or badge and maybe an ongoing role working alongside adult detectives.

Radio Green Oaks chattered in the background as she watched the blank faces of the people gliding in and out of the banks. She watched people draw hundreds of pounds out, as if in a daze. A young couple each with five or six carrier bags from the fashion stores floated over, withdrew £100 each and then drifted back towards the shops. Their glassiness was part of a wider unreal feeling in the centre. No one appeared to have a purpose; they would drift into Kate's path and then block her way, seeming to just walk on the spot. Sometimes it scared her. She thought she might be the only living thing in Green Oaks. Other times she thought that perhaps she was a ghost haunting the lanes and escalators.

She knew that one day she would see someone by the banks with a different look on their face. Anxiety, or cunning, or hate, or desire, and she would know that they were a suspect. So she scanned the faces for any flicker of deviance. Her eyes moved over the play area where there were some children her own age looking unimpressed with the facilities. They were too old for the jungle fantasy and the ball pool, but unlike Kate they didn't seem to realize that the whole centre was an enormous playground. She felt the dull ache of loneliness in her stomach, but her brain didn't register it. It was old news.

Kate's favourite book, *How to be a Detective* (part of the Junior Factfinder series), was quite explicit about the sore feet and boredom necessary to crack crime. You had to put the hours in all day, every day:

The best detectives are always prepared – day or night. They can be called upon at any time to investigate crimes or follow suspects. Crooks are cunning and love the cover of darkness.

It was classified top-secret information, but Kate had spent a night at Green Oaks. She'd typed a note home about a fabricated school trip away and had set off with Mickey, a flask and her notebook. She got to the centre just before it closed and hid in the little plastic house in the middle of the children's play area. She waited there, until the shop-workers went home and the muzak was turned off. She'd tried to stay awake all night, watching the banks from inside the house, getting out every now and then to take a closer look and stretch her legs. She must have fallen asleep just before dawn; when she woke up the banks were open and the first customers were already there. Luckily Mickey, professional as ever, had remained alert, so nothing had been missed. She was disappointed with her lack of stamina though. She was determined to try again and next time to stay awake all night.

The man sitting two seats away got up and walked away and Kate realized with annoyance that he had been sitting there for a long time, but that she hadn't seen his face. Maybe he was casing Lloyds, maybe his face showed a concentrated expression. She got up to follow him, but changed her mind when she realized she should be getting home. She put an entry for her surveillance shift into her notebook, stuffed Mickey's head back into her bag and headed for the bus.

YOUNG STALIN

by **Simon Sebag Montefiore**

W&N

YOUNG STALIN

by **Simon Sebag Montefiore**

Stalin, like Hitler, remains the personification of evil but also one of the creators of today's world. Based on massive research and astonishing new evidence in archives from Moscow to Georgia, 'Young Stalin' is a chronicle of the Revolution, a pre-history of the USSR and an intimate biography unveiling the shadowy, adventurous journey of the Georgian cobbler's son who was to become the Red Tsar.

Simon Sebag Montefiore *is a historian and writer. 'Young Stalin' is the prequel and companion to 'Stalin: The Court of the Red Tsar' which won the History Book of the Year Prize at the 2004 British Book Awards. A Fellow of the Royal Society of Literature, novelist, and television presenter, Montefiore lives in London with his wife, the novelist Santa Montefiore, and their two children.*

"Everything you could ask for from a biography – exhaustive research, a compelling subject and a beautifully written narrative that will endure as a portrait of one of the towering figures of modern history."

Judges
Danny Danziger – Writer and columnist
Emma Jepson – Non-Fiction Buyer, Borders
Stephanie Merritt – Journalist and novelist

To my darling son Sasha

Morning

The rose's bud had blossomed out
Reaching out to touch the violet
The lily was waking up
And bending its head in the breeze

High in the clouds the lark
Was singing a chirruping hymn
While the joyful nightingale
With a gentle voice was saying –

'Be full of blossom, oh lovely land
Rejoice Iverians' country
And you oh Georgian, by studying
Bring joy to your motherland.'

SOSELO

(Josef Stalin)

I

KEKE'S MIRACLE: SOSO

On 17 May 1872, a handsome young cobbler, the very model of a chivalrous Georgian man, Vissarion 'Beso' Djugashvili, aged twenty-two, married Ekaterina 'Keke' Geladze, seventeen, an attractive freckled girl with auburn hair, at the Uspensky Church in the small Georgian town of Gori.

A matchmaker had visited Keke's house to tell her about the suit of Beso the cobbler: he was a respected artisan in Baramov's small workshop, quite a catch. 'Beso', says Keke in newly discovered memoirs,* 'was considered a very popular young man among my friends and they were all dreaming of marrying him. My friends nearly burst with jealousy. Beso was an enviable groom, a true *karachogheli* [Georgian knight], with beautiful moustaches, very well dressed – and with the special sophistication of a town-dweller.' Nor was Keke in any doubt that she herself was something of a catch too: 'Among my female friends, I became the desired and beautiful girl.' Indeed, 'slender, chestnut-haired with big eyes', she was said to be 'very pretty'.

The wedding, according to tradition, took place just after sunset; Georgian social life, writes one historian, was 'as ritualised as English Victorian behaviour'. The marriage was celebrated with the rambunctious festivity of the wild town of Gori. 'It was', Keke remembers, 'hugely glamorous.' The male guests were true *karachogheli*, 'cheerful, daring and generous', wearing their splendid black *chokhas*, 'broad-shouldered with slim waists.' The chief of Beso's two best men was Yakov 'Koba' Egnatashvili, a strapping wrestler, wealthy merchant and local

*The memoirs have lain in the Georgian Communist Party archive, forgotten for seventy years. They were never used in the Stalinist cult. It seems Stalin neither read them nor knew they existed because, as far as this author can learn, they were not sent to Stalin's Moscow archives. He did not want his mother's views published. When Keke was interviewed Hello! – magazine style in 1935 in the Soviet press, Stalin furiously reprimanded the Politburo: 'I ask you to forbid the Philistine riffraff that has penetrated our press from publishing any more "interviews" with my mother and all other crass publicity. I ask you to spare me from the importunate sensationalism of these scoundrels!' Keke, always strongwilled and unimpressed with her son's power, must have recorded them secretly and in defiance of him on 23 – 27 August 1935 shortly before her death.

hero who, as Keke puts it, 'always tried to assist us in the creation of our family'.

The groom and his friends gathered for toasts at his home, before parading through the streets to collect Keke and her family. The garlanded couple then rode to church together in a colourfully decorated wedding phaeton, bells tingling, ribbons fluttering. In the church, the choir gathered in the gallery; below them, men and women stood separately among the flickering candles. The singers burst into their elevating and harmonic Georgian melodies accompanied by a *zurna*, a Georgian wind instrument like a Berber pipe.

The bride entered with her bridesmaids, who were careful not to tread on the train, a special augur of bad luck. Father Khakhanov, an Armenian, conducted the ceremony, Father Kasradze recorded the marriage, and Father Christopher Charkviani, a family friend, sang so finely that Yakov Egnatashvili 'generously tipped him 10 roubles', no mean sum. Afterwards, Beso's friends headed the traditional singing and dancing procession through the streets, playing *duduki*, long pipes, to the *supra*, a Georgian feast presided over by a *tamada*, a joke-telling and wisdom-imparting toastmaster.

The service and singing had been in the unique Georgian language – not Russian because Georgia was only a recent addition to the Romanov Empire. For a thousand years, ruled by scions of the Bagratoni dynasty, the Kingdom of Sakartvelo (Georgia to Westerners, Gruzia to Russians) was an independent Christian bulwark of knightly valour against the Islamic Mongol, Timurid, Ottoman and Persian Empires. Its apogee was the twelfth-century empire of Queen Tamara, made timeless by the national epic, *The Knight in the Panther Skin* by Rustaveli. Over the centuries, the kingdom splintered into bickering principalities. In 1801 and 1810, the Tsars Paul and Alexander I annexed principalities to their empire. The Russians had only finished the military conquest of the Caucasus with the surrender of Imam Shamyl and his Chechen warriors in 1859 after a thirty-year war – and Adjaria, the last slice of Georgia, was gained in 1878. Even the most aristocratic Georgians, who served at the courts of the Emperor in St Petersburg or of the Viceroy in Tiflis, dreamed of independence. Hence Keke's pride in following Georgian traditions of manhood and marriage.

Beso, mused Keke, *'appeared* to be a good family man ... He believed in God and always went to church.' The parents of both bride and groom had been serfs of local princes, freed in the 1860s by the Tsar-Liberator, Alexander II. Beso's grandfather, Zaza, was an Ossetian* from the village of Geri, north of Gori. Zaza, like Stalin, his great-grandson, became a Georgian rebel: in 1804, he joined the uprising of Prince Elizbar Eristavi against Russia. Afterwards, he was settled with other 'baptized Ossetians' in the village of Didi-Lilo, 9 miles from Tiflis, as a serf of Prince Badur Machabeli. Zaza's son Vano tended the Prince's vineyards and had two sons, Giorgi, who was murdered by bandits, and Beso, who got a job in Tiflis in the shoe factory of G. G. Adelkhanov but was headhunted by the Armenian Josef Baramov to make boots for the Russian garrison in Gori. There young Beso noticed the 'fascinating, neatly dressed girl with chestnut hair and beautiful eyes.'

Keke was also new to Gori, a daughter of Glakho Geladze, a peasant serf of the local granee, Prince Amilakhvari. Her father worked as a potter near by before becoming the gardener for a wealthy Armenian, Zakhar Gambarov, who owned fine gardens at Gambareuli on Gori's outskirts. As her father died young, Keke was raised by her mother's family. She remembered the excitement of moving to unruly Gori: 'What a happy journey it was! Gori was festively decorated, crowds of people swelled like

*The Ossetians were a semi-pagan mountain people who lived on the northern borders of Georgia proper, some becoming assimilated Georgians though most remain proudly separate: in 1991 – 3, south Ossetians fought the Georgians and are now autonomous. When Stalin's dying father was admitted to hospital, significantly he was still registered as Ossetian. Stalin's enemies, from Trotsky to the poet Mandelstam in his famous poem, relished calling him an 'Ossete' because Georgians regarded Ossetians as barbarous, crude and, in the early nineteenth century, non-Christian. Djugashvili certainly sounds as if it has an Ossetian root: it means 'son of Djuga' in Georgian. Stalin's mother says Beso told her the name was based on the Georgian djogi or 'herd' root because they were herdsmen and were driven out of Geri by marauding Ossetians. The real relevance is lost because, by the time of Stalin's birth, the Djugashvilis were totally Georgianized. Stalin himself wrote about this: 'What is to be done with the Ossetians ...becoming assimilated by the Georgians?'

the sea. A military parade dazzled our eyes. Music blared. *Sazandari* [a band of four percussion and wind instruments], and sweet *duduki* played, and everyone sang.'

Her young husband was a thin dark figure with black eyebrows and moustaches, always sporting a black Circassian coat, tightly belted, a peaked cap and baggy trousers tucked into high boots. 'Unusual, peculiar and morose', but also 'clever and proud', Beso was able to speak four languages (Georgian, Russian, Turkish and Armenian) and quote *The Knight in the Panther Skin*.

The Djugashvilis prospered. Many houses in Gori were so poor they were made of mud and dug out of the earth. But for the wife of the busy cobbler Beso there was no fear of such poverty. 'Our family happiness', declared Keke, 'was limitless.'

Beso 'left Baramov to open his own workshop', backed by his friends, especially his patron Egnatashvili, who bought him the 'machine-tools'. Keke was soon pregnant. 'Many married couples would envy our family happiness.' Indeed, her marriage to the desired Beso still caused jealousy among her contemporaries: 'evil tongues didn't stop even after the marriage'. It is interesting that Keke stresses this gossip: perhaps someone else had expected to marry Beso. Whether or not Keke stole him from another fiancée, 'evil tongues', later citing the best man Egnatashvili, the priest Charkviani, Gori's police officer Damian Davrichewy and a host of celebrities and aristocrats, started wagging early in the marriage.

ↀ

Just over nine months after the wedding, on 14 February 1875, 'our happiness was marked by the birth of our son. Yakov Egnatashvili helped us so very much.' Egnatashvili stood godfather and 'Beso laid on a grand christening. Beso was almost mad with happiness.' But two months later the little boy, named Mikheil, died. 'Our happiness turned to sorrow. Beso started to drink from grief.' Keke fell pregnant again. A second son, Giorgi, was born on 24 December 1876. Again Egnatashvili stood godfather, again unluckily. The baby died of measles on 19 June 1877.

'Our happiness was shattered.' Beso was manic with grief and blamed 'the icon of Geri', the shrine of his home village. The couple had appealed to the icon for the life of their child. Keke's mother Melania started visiting fortune-tellers. Beso kept drinking. The icon of St George was brought into the house. They climbed the Gorijvari mountain, towering over the town, to pray in the church that stood beside the medieval fortress. Keke fell pregnant for the third time and swore that, if the child survived, she would go on pilgrimage to Geri to thank God for the miracle of St George. On 6 December 1878, she gave birth to a third son.*

'We sped up the christening so he wouldn't die unchristened.' Keke cared for him in the poky two-room one-storey cottage that contained little except a samovar, bed, divan, table and kerosene lamp. A small trunk held almost all the family's belongings. Spiral stairs led down to the musky cellar with three niches, one for Beso's tools, one for Keke's sewing-kit and one for the fire. There Keke tended the baby's cot. The family lived on the basic Georgian fare: *lobio* beans, *badridjani* aubergine and thick *lavashi* bread. Only rarely did they eat *mtsvadi*, Georgian shashlik.

On 17 December the baby was christened Josef, known as Soso – the boy who would become Stalin. Soso was 'weak, fragile, thin', said his mother. 'If there was a bug, he was sure to catch it first.' The second and third toes of his left foot were webbed.

Beso decided not to ask the family's benefactor Egnatashvili to be godfather. 'Yakov's hand was unlucky,' said Beso, but even if the merchant missed the church formalities, Stalin and his mother always called him 'godfather Yakov'.

Keke's mother reminded Beso that they had sworn to take a pilgrimage to the church at Geri if the baby lived. 'Just let the child survive,' answered Beso, 'and I'll crawl to Geri on my knees

---

*Stalin later invented much about his life: his official birthday was 21 December 1879, over a year later, an invented date. He generally stuck to 6 December 1878 until an interview in 1920 with a Swedish newspaper. In 1925, he ordered his secretary Tovstukha to formalize the 1879 date. There are several explanations, including his desire to recreate himself. Most likely, he moved the date later to avoid conscription. As for the house where he was born, this is the hovel that now stands alone on Gori's Stalin Boulevard, surrounded by the Grecian temple built during the 1930s by Stalin's Caucasian viceroy and later secret police chief, Lavrenti Beria, next to the cathedral-like Stalin Museum. The Djugashvilis did not live there long.

with the child on my shoulders!' But he delayed it until the child caught another chill which shocked him into prayer: they travelled to Geri, 'facing much hardship on the way, donated a sheep, and ordered a thanksgiving service there'. But the Geri priests were conducting an exorcism, holding a little girl over a precipice to drive out evil spirits. Keke's baby 'was horrified and screamed', and they returned to Gori where little Stalin 'shuddered and raved even in his sleep' – but he lived and became his mother's beloved treasure.

'Keke didn't have enough milk', so her son also shared the breasts of the wives of Tsikhatatrishvili (his formal godfather) and Egnatashvili. 'At first the baby didn't accept my mother's milk,' says Alexander Tsikhatatrishvili, ' but gradually he liked it providing he covered his eyes so he couldn't see my mother.' Sharing the milk of the Egnatashvili children made them 'like milk brothers with Soso', says Galina Djugashvili, Stalin's granddaughter.

Soso started to speak early. He loved flowers and music, especially when Keke's brothers Gio and Sandala played the *duduki* pipes. The Georgians love to sing and Stalin never lost his enjoyment of the haunting Georgian melodies.* In later life, he remembered hearing the 'Georgian men singing on their way to market'.

Beso's little business was flourishing – he took on apprentices and as many as ten employees. One of the apprentices, Dato Gasitashvili, who loved Soso and helped bring him up, recalled Beso's prosperity: 'He lived better than anyone else of our profession. They always had butter in their house.' There were later whispers about this prosperity, embarrassing for a proletarian hero. 'I'm not the son of a worker,' Stalin admitted. 'My father had a shoe workshop, employing apprentices, an exploiter. We didn't live badly.' It was during this happy time that Keke became friends with Maria and Arshak Ter-Petrossian, a wealthy Armenian military contractor, whose son Simon would become infamous as the bank-robber Kamo.

*Stalin the dictator became a keen gardener, growing lemons, tomatoes and above all roses and mimosas. His favourite Georgian songs were 'Fly Away Black Swallow' and 'Suliko'.

Keke adored her child and 'in old age, I still can see his first steps, a vision that burns like a candle'. She and her mother taught him to walk by exploiting his love of flowers: Keke would hold out a camomile, and Soso ran to grasp it. When she took Soso to a wedding, he noticed a flower in the bride's veil and grabbed it. Keke told him off but godfather Egnatashvili lovingly 'kissed the child and caressed him, saying, "if even now you want to steal the bride, God knows what you'll do when you're older."'

Soso's survival seemed miraculous to the grateful mother. 'How happy we were, how we laughed!' reminisces Keke. Her reverence must have instilled in Soso a sense of specialness: the Freudian dictum that the mother's devotion made him feel like a conqueror was undoubtedly true. 'Soselo', as she lovingly called him, grew up super-sensitive but also displayed a masterful confidence from an early age.

Yet at the height of Beso's success there was a shadow: his clients paid him partly in wine which was so plentiful in Georgia that many workers received alcohol instead of cash. Furthermore, he did some business in the corner of a friend's *dukhan* (tavern), which encouraged him to drink too much. Beso befriended a drinking partner, a Russian political exile named Poka, possibly a *narodnik* populist or a radical connected to the People's Will, the terrorists who were at that time repeatedly attempting to assassinate Emperor Alexander II. So Stalin grew up knowing a Russian revolutionary. 'My son made friends with him,' says Keke, 'and Poka bought him a canary.' But the Russian was a hopeless alcoholic who lived in rags. One winter, he was found dead in the snow.

Beso found he 'could not stop drinking. A good family man was destroyed,' declares Keke. The booze started to ruin the business: 'his hands began shaking and he couldn't sew shoes. The business was only kept going by his apprentices.'

Learning nothing from Poka's demise, Beso acquired a new boon drinking companion in the priest Charkviani. Provincial Georgia was priest-ridden, but these men of God enjoyed their worldly pleasures. Once church services were over, the priests spent much of their time drinking wine in Gori's taverns until they were blind drunk. As an old man, Stalin remembered: 'As soon as Father Charkviani finished his service, he dropped in and the two men hurried to the *dukhan*.'* They returned home leaning on each other, hugging and 'singing out of tune', totally sozzled.

'You're a good bloke, Beso, even for a shoemaker,' drawled the priest.

'You're a priest, but what a priest, I love you!' wheezed Beso. The two drunks would embrace. Keke begged Father Charkviani not to take Beso drinking. Keke and her mother beseeched Beso to stop. So did Egnatashvili, but that did not help – probably because of the rumours already spreading around town.

Perhaps these were the same 'evil tongues' Keke mentioned at the wedding because Josef Davrichewy, the son of Gori's police chief, claims in his memoirs that 'the birth was gossiped about in the neighbourhood – that the real father of child was Koba Egnatashvili ... or my own father Damian Davrichewy'. This could not have helped Beso, whom Davrichewy calls 'a manically jealous runt', already sinking into alcoholism.

৩

In the course of 1883, Beso became 'touchy and very careless', getting into drunken fights and earning the nickname 'Crazy Beso'.

Paternity suits develop proportional to the power and fame of the child. Once Stalin became Soviet dictator, his rumoured fathers included the celebrated Central Asian explorer Nikolai Przhevalsky, who resembled the adult Stalin and passed through Gori, and even the future Emperor Alexander III himself, who had visited Tiflis, supposedly staying at a palace where Keke toiled as a maid. But the explorer was a homosexual who was not near Georgia when Stalin was conceived, while Keke was not in Tiflis at the same time as the Tsarevich.

---

*These Georgian inns 'provide nothing but unfurnished and dirty rooms, bread (with cheese), tea, wine and at best eggs and poultry', warns Baedeker. 'Those who wish for meat must buy a whole sheep (4-5 roubles) or sucking pig (2-3 roubles).'

Leaving aside these absurdities, who was Stalin's real father? Egnatashvili was indeed the patron of the family, comforter of the wife and sponsor of the son. He was married with children, lived affluently, owned several flourishing taverns and was a prosperous wine-dealer in a country that virtually floated on wine. More than that, this strapping athlete with the waxed moustaches was a champion wrestler in a town that worshipped fighters. As already noted, Keke herself writes that he 'always tried to assist us in the creation of our family', an unfortunate but perhaps revealing turn of phrase. It seems unlikely she meant it literally – or was she trying to tell us something?

Davrichewy the police chief, who helped Keke when she complained about her husband's unruly drinking, was another potential father: 'as far I know, Soso was the natural son of Davrichewy,' testified Davrichewy's friend Jourouli, the town's mayor. 'Everyone in Gori knew about his affair with Soso's pretty mother.

Stalin himself once said his father was really a priest, which brings us to the third candidate, Father Charkviani. Egnatashvili, Davrichewy and Charkviani were all married, but in Georgia's macho culture, men were almost expected to keep mistresses, like their Italian brethren. Gori's priests were notoriously debauched. All three were prominent local men who enjoyed rescuing a pretty young wife in trouble.

As for Keke herself, it has always been hard to match the pious old lady in her black nunnish headdress of the 1930s with the irrepressible young woman of the 1880s. Her piety is not in doubt, but religious observance has never ruled out sins of the flesh. She certainly took pride in being 'the desired and beautiful girl' and there is evidence that she was much more worldly than she appeared. As an old lady, Keke supposedly encouraged Nina Beria, wife of Lavrenti, Stalin's Caucasian viceroy, to take lovers and talked very spicily about sexual matters: 'When I was young, I cleaned house for people and when I met a good-looking boy, I didn't waste the opportunity.' The Berias are hostile witnesses, but there is a hint of earthy mischief even in Keke's memoirs. In her garden, she recounts, her mother managed to attract Soso with a flower, at which Keke jovially pulled out her breasts and showed them to the toddler who ignored the flower and dived for the breasts. But the drunken Russian exile Poka was spying on them and burst out laughing, so 'I buttoned up my dress'.

Stalin, in his elliptical, mendacious way, encouraged these stories. When he chatted in his last years to a Georgian protégé Mgeladze, he gave him 'the impression that he was Egnatashvili's illegitimate son' and seemed to deny he was Beso's. At a reception in 1934, he specifically said, 'My father was a priest.' But in Beso's absence, all three paternal candidates helped bring him up: he lived with the Charkvianis, was protected by the Davrichewys and spent half his time at the Egnatashvili's, so he surely felt filial fondness for them. There was another reason for the priest rumour: the Church School accepted only the children of clergy, so his mother says he was passed off as the son of a priest.

Stalin remained ambiguous about Crazy Beso: he despised him, but he also showed pride and sympathy too. They had some happy moments. Beso told Soso stories of Georgia's heroic outlaws who 'fought against the rich, stole from princes to help peasants'. At hard-drinking dinners, Stalin the dictator boasted to Khrushchev and other magnates that he had inherited his father's head for alcohol. His father had fed him wine off his fingertips in his cot, and he insisted on doing the same with his own children, much to the fury of his wife Nadya. Later he wrote touchingly about an anonymous shoemaker with a small workshop, ruined by cruel capitalism. 'The wings of his dreams', he wrote, were 'clipped'. He once bragged that 'my father could make two pairs of shoes in a single day' and, even as a dictator, liked to call himself a shoemaker too. He later used the name 'Besoshvili' – Son of Beso – as an alias, and his closest Gori friends called him 'Beso'.

Weighing up all these stories, it is most likely that Stalin was the son of Beso despite the drunkard's rantings about Soso as a 'bastard'. A married woman was always expected to be respectable, but it is hardly outrageous if the pretty young

Keke, a semi-widow, did become the mistress of Egnatashvili when her marriage disintegrated. In her memoirs, Egnatashvili appears as often as her husband, and is remembered much more fondly. She does say that he was so kind and helpful to her that it caused a certain 'awkwardness'. Some of the Egnatashvili family claim there was a 'genetic' connection with Stalin. However, Egnatashvili's grandson, Guram Ratishvili, puts it best: 'We simply do not know if he was Stalin's father, but we *do* know that the merchant became the boy's substitute father.'

Rumours of bastardy, like those of Ossetian origins, were another way of diminishing the tyrant Stalin, widely hated in Georgia, which he conquered and repressed in the 1920s. It is true that great men of humble origins are often said to be the sons of other men. Yet sometimes they really are the offspring of their official fathers.

'When he was young,' testified a schoolfriend, David Papitashvili, Stalin 'closely resembled his father'. As he got older, says Alexander Tsikhatatrishvili, 'he looked more and more like his father and when he grew his moustache, they looked identical.'

By the time Soso was five, Crazy Beso was an alcoholic tormented by paranoia and prone to violence. 'Day by day,' said Keke, 'it got worse'.

TILT

by **Jean Sprackland**

TILT

by **Jean Sprackland**

Jean Sprackland's third collection describes a world in freefall. Chaos and calamity are at our shoulder, in the shape of fire and flood, ice-storm and hurricane; trains stand still, zoos are abandoned, migrating birds lose their way – all surfaces are unreliable, all territories unmapped. These poems explore the ambivalence and dark unease of slippage and collapse, but also carry a powerful sense of the miraculous made manifest amongst the ordinary.

***Jean Sprackland's** first collection of poetry, 'Tattoos for Mothers Day', was shortlisted for the Forward Prize for Best First Collection in 1999. Her second collection, 'Hard Water', was published by Cape in 2003 and shortlisted for the T.S. Eliot Award and the Whitbread Poetry Award. In 2004, Jean Sprackland was named by the Poetry Book Society as one of the 'Next Generation' poets.*

"A great collection – crafted and delicate poems that tell us what it is to be alive now."

Judges
Sion Hamilton – Ground Floor Manager, Foyles
Vicki Feaver – Poet and painter
Adam Phillips – Psychoanalyst and writer

THE FENCED WOOD

A finger of sunlight points the way
over the floor of dead leaves.
I unlatch the gate and walk in.

I follow the signs:
an acorn
a notched twig
a word written in lichen.

At the centre
a flat stone for a bed.
I lie down to wait.
The cold receives me.
The net of light trembles overhead.

One branch touches the wrist of another.
The breeze catches its breath.

BIRTHDAY POEM

A roll of blue silk
left on the edge of the counter.

Silk. Edge. Under the fluorescent light
that frail equation shimmered. Then

the silk shifted, or the spool relinquished it –

unsleeving
slowly at first, then
gathering confidence
spending itself faster
and faster, a torrent
flashing over and pooling beneath –

and dragged the spool thumping to the floor.
The assistant turned, too late.

Halfway through my life I think of it.
That roll of shining stuff.
Its choice to spill.
Acceleration. Rapture.

HANDS

She peels cod fillets off the slab,
dips them in batter, drops them
one by one into the storm of hot fat.
I watch her scrubbed hands,
elegant at the work

and think of the hands of the midwife
stroking wet hair from my face as I sobbed and cursed,
calling me Sweetheart and wheeling in more gas,
hauling out at last my slippery fish of a son.
He was all silence and milky blue. She took him away
and brought him back breathing,
wrapped in a white sheet. By then
I loved her like my own mother.

I stand here speechless in the steam and banter,
as she makes hospital corners of my hot paper parcel.

CATCH ME

Hold a warm condom to the light
to see the fund of life inside.

Not so long ago
the only place to hold this was the body,
its channels and propagation chambers,
and pleasure was taken ripe with consequence.

And once there were no vessels
and no containment.
No fashioning of wood or stone
into a jug to carry water –
water had to be visited, drunk where it lived,
paths marked to those holy places.
No rooms to fill with music,
no music to carry longing or grief
but wind, thunder, animal cries.

Then came the mud house,
the leaky bowl of leaves.
We learned like children to keep and store,
to build edges and own space.
And later one of us said to the other
I'm everywhere, I'm lost, catch me,
make your arms into walls and hold me.

"THE MAP IS NOT THE TERRITORY"

(Alfred Korzybski)

The pirates would swarm aboard
slashing throats and seizing the maps.
Without maps, all the black pepper, all the slaves
might as well be thrown into the sea.

But maps could lie. Under the spitting lantern
the mapmaker practised a dark art,
drawing up insurance against loss.
Invented a safe route onto lethal rocks.
Marked a green island where there was nothing
but empty blue road under a ratcheting sun.

Unthinkable now, we are so correct
with our clean atlas of distant starfields

and even the body mapped –
its fabric unpicked, its algorithms read,
every nub and rubric imaged and modelled,
down to the last glisten of stuff.

Each of our diagrams is as true
as we know how to make it.
No trap street, no bit of bad code.

So how will we hold something back
when they board us and raid us?

MATTRESSES

Tipped down the embankment, they
sprawl like sloshed suburban wives,

buckled and split, slashed by rain,
moulded by bodies dead or disappeared
and reeking with secrets.

A lineside museum of sleep and sex,
an archive of thrills and emissions,
the histories of half-lives
spent hiding in the dark.

Arthritic iron frames might still be worth a bit,
but never that pink quilted headboard,
naked among thistles, relic
of some reckless beginning, testament

to the usual miracle: the need to be close,
whatever the stains or the bruises.

THE BIRKDALE NIGHTINGALE

(Bufo calamito – the Natterjack toad)

On Spring nights you can hear them
two miles away, calling their mates
to the breeding place, a wet slack in the dunes.
Lovers hiding nearby are surprised
by desperate music. One man searched all night
for a crashed spaceship.

For amphibians, they are terrible swimmers:
where it's tricky to get ashore, they drown.
By day they sleep in crevices under the boardwalk,
run like lizards from cover to cover
without the sense to leap when a gull snaps.
Yes, he can make himself fearsome,
inflating his lungs to double his size.
But cars on the coast road are not deterred.

She will lay a necklace of pearls in the reeds.
Next morning, a dog will run into the water and scatter them.
Or she'll spawn in a footprint filled with salt rain
that will dry to a crust in two days.

Still, when he calls her and climbs her
they are well designed. The nuptial pads on his thighs
velcro him to her back. She steadies beneath him.

The puddle brims with moonlight.
Everything leads to this.

DAY

by **A. L. Kennedy**

DAY

by **A. L. Kennedy**

Alfred Day wanted his war. In its turmoil he found his proper purpose as the tail-gunner in a Lancaster bomber; he found the wild, dark fellowship of his crew, and he found Joyce, a woman to love. But that's all gone now – the war took it away. Now, in 1949, Alfred is winding back time to see where he lost himself. He has taken the role of an extra in a POW film. Shipped out to Germany and an ersatz camp, he picks his way through the clichés that will become all that's left of his war and begins to do what he's never dared – to remember. He is looking for some semblance of hope: trying to move forward by going back.

A.L. Kennedy is a novelist and stand-up comedian. She has published four previous novels, two books of non-fiction, and three collections of short stories, most recently 'Indelible Acts'. She has twice been selected as one of Granta's Best of Young British Novelists and has won a number of prizes including the Somerset Maugham Award, the Encore Award and the Saltire Scottish Book of the Year Award. She lives in Glasgow.

"Although it could have been any one of our shortlist of four, we chose A.L. Kennedy as our winner because, through an extraordinary act of ventriloquism, she describes the waste and eventual resurrection of a young life shattered by war. This book is a masterpiece."

Judges
Sam Leith – Literary Editor, Daily Telegraph
Nigel Rees – Writer and broadcaster
Polly Samson – Author and lyricist

DAY

That had been his letter-writing pen. His lucky pen. Notes to his ma: tell her where he was, give her the happiest version of how he was getting along, and then suddenly more, needing words that hadn't been invented, words he didn't know were already hiding, ready in his skin.

Letters to Joyce.

Real letters, and a fight to make them carry what they should, not to scare her, but to keep her, not to love her too plainly, but to touch her enough.

Apologise for the terrible handwriting and check on the spelling of everything and the commas, apostrophes, all the punctuation, practically each fucking chicken scratch that made it to the paper, he'd study and puzzle at because she'd be sure to notice his mistakes and think him stupid, half soaked. She wouldn't say so, but she'd know he wasn't right for her.

Joyce.

The finest thing you hide the longest.

But what am I hiding now? Only that she's gone.

Off with someone else.

I think.

Didn't want me, anyway – with or without someone else.

But it had seemed that she did.

She'd been there before the crew, before the skipper. Back when his days were full of unfamiliar pawls and pins and springs and learning silhouettes, stripping mechanisms, feed opening components, judging wingspans, angles of attack. The bod who taught them aircraft recognition gave them slide shows – Me 109s and FW 190s and girlie shots mixed in to hold their interest, which Alfred didn't think much of. There you were trying to be quick, knowing you had to be, concentrating, and then you're studying some dancing girl's tits, or some Jane Russell-type of bint smirking past you, it muddled your feelings: that restlessness to do with firing and your memory already too tight and thinking of the magic-lantern shows in the chapel Sunday school and a sweat rising under your knees at so much flesh which you had never seen in life and did not think you ever would.

Except in London – everyone got everything in London. You'd heard about that. In gossip, in jokes, in personal health and hygiene lectures, you'd heard about that. It was all on offer there – hooch and private clubs and dreadful diseases and women selling it in the streets, professionals and amateurs out round Piccadilly Circus and dreadful diseases and Soho – God help you in Soho – and dreadful diseases and nicer girls in dances and maybe WAAFs – you were slightly used to WAAFs – and when you were a man in uniform, you could do quite well. If you didn't worry, if you didn't think about guilt and the dreadful diseases and imagine you might be doomed from the very start, then you might let yourself be talked into going and even be hardly surprised when you stroll off the train at King's Cross station and really are there – in London, with a bit of money and looking quite fine for a short-arse in your Best Blue and not everything about you is so very short, as it turns out – another thing you've learned in uniform – so you've no cause for dejection and there you are, all equipped for most things you can think of – which isn't much – and up in bloody London.

Which meant Alfred, with his forty-eight-hour pass, had gone with four gunnery training mates to his nation's capital and seat of government, because they all had to go and try their luck.

Looking for an easy way to test it – no harm meant and no ammunition required.

Although two of the lads had girls there and family and they pretty much disappeared once they'd supped a pint and made everyone come down Putney way because that was convenient for their houses, even if it meant that Alfred didn't see the sights – or not so that he noticed – only bombed-out buildings here and there and a patch of the river.

Once the Putney lads had gone Alfred was left with a bloke known as Ditcher – although he'd never ditched – and a quiet type called Blamey, none of them sure of where they were once they'd walked a bit off from the pub in London's odd, charged dark, a fat moon lifting overhead. They'd walked back towards the Thames, they hoped, in a chilly night and had gone far enough to be highly browned off with not finding it when Blamey hailed a cab and a car did stop – but maybe not a cab – and in got Ditcher and Blamey and then, before they could do a thing about it, some other chap had climbed in after from the off side and everyone shouting as the doors slammed and the car drove clean away.

Which left Alfred in the dark and sobering rapidly. He gave up on the river, then found it, crossed it, wandered along by himself fretting he should have used this time to see his ma, check that her letters weren't phoney and she really was doing all right.

He'd not been clear about where his party had hoped they'd spend the night – the YMCA, a French madam's boudoir and requesting a serviceman's discount at the Ritz had all been mentioned. He was beginning to feel lonesome, childish, tricked, but then Goering took a hand and the sirens went up for a raid, the hot columns of searchlights starting to topple and sweep, ticking round for bombers.

They look for our boys, we look for theirs.

He'd stumbled on the right way for a shelter: one of the brick-built ones that looked a shoddy job, materials skimped, which was funny, because the area seemed presentable from what he could tell in the whining black. He remembered thinking one direct hit would knock down the whole lousy effort. But maybe serve them right – maybe they'd demanded a local shelter – could you do that, if you'd got the money, influence? Seemed you could do most things if you were that kind – the five courses at the Ritz and bugger the rationing kind – so why not demand somewhere for yourself, or maybe for your staff, if you didn't just run for your country house and stay there in a funk?

Count on a war to bring out the finest in people.

He went inside anyway, perhaps out of curiosity – and because if your number's up, it's up, and you could be sitting in a fine, deep Underground station and have a sewer blown apart above you and then drown as easy as anything, choke in shit, or maybe you'd only fall on the steps going down and crush yourself, crush everybody, no matter what you were worth.

He'd turned through the blast protection and then been knocked against the wall. Couldn't work out for a moment why he'd never heard the bomb – then realised this bundle had swiped round and clocked him when he wasn't expecting it. This bundle carried by a woman's voice.

'I'm so sorry. Did I hurt you?'

But she hadn't hurt him, he was only surprised. 'No, I'm –' And the bundle unravelling then and dropping: a quilt, a book in a plain paper jacket, a glasses case, a packet that suggested sandwiches.

I wanted to know what book. Already trying to know people by their books. Stupid habit.

She'd managed to keep hold of her Thermos. 'Thank the Lord.' Joyce. 'Oh, dear.' Standing close, almost against her – like being, all at once, in a warm room and happy. Joyce.

Green coat buttoned to the top and her hair not exactly brushed, very deep black, and the largest eyes, these huge dark eyes. Joyce. He sees her and feels untroubled, slowed.

She was a place to live. My place to live.

Joyce. And already he's looking too much and can't stop, but she hasn't noticed, is busy with flustering over her things, so he'll just keep on. Even when he crouches to help her he keeps on, takes in her shoes – good but scuffed – and her ankles, her legs, the start of her legs, the calves, the way they take his thinking out of words and into a panic: thin, thin, dizzy air.

He hands up the case for her glasses but doesn't lift his head, because he is blushing and appalled. He wants to run somewhere with her. And he wants a few days to consider, to gather himself. And he wants things he cannot say.

'Oh, that's – You're most awfully kind.'

Felt like a creature, a wammell. Heat and shame and enjoying the shame. Hotter because of it.

Raising the quilt that is warm from her arms and heavy and sweet-scented, he stands and he folds it and can't think if he should hold it tight or else far away from himself, because both of the choices would seem rude.

And you're a good boy, remember. Hold hard on to that.

And now that he's standing, it's her turn to bend at his feet which staggers him again, the glimpse of her bared neck, while she gathers up her book. He worries that he smells of beer, of the twist in his head, of this new, marvellous burning.

And then because he's a fool and he does want to know what book, 'That's a long . . . a big . . . What are you reading?'

Shy about it when she answers, 'Oh. It's, you know, *The Odyssey of Homer* – new translation. I never really paid attention when I was at school. Bit of a dummy. I'm up to where Circe turns them into pigs.'

And his face dying, abandoned out there in front of his thinking, because he cannot nod as if he's read it, cannot move, and soon she will raise her eyes, stop staring at the wallpaper cover she's used to protect her book – she takes care of books – and she will see that he's just an idiot and they've nothing in common at all.

'Anyway, I remember he gets home safe in the end, gets the girl and so forth . . .'

The end of her sentence tingling in his spine.

And not sure if she was making it sound simple, because then I'd understand – her being kind – or if that was only her way of talking. She seemed kind. Always kind.

She clears her throat neatly and begins edging further into the shelter, chattering on as she draws him in behind her. 'I don't usually come here – been using the basement, because it lasted through the proper Blitz, so why not. Only then the house two doors along caught it last week and their basement didn't come off very well.' He thinks, hopes, she hasn't noticed he's so much a bloody fool.

And they're walking together after that and finding a space, sitting, this old dear frowning at them sideways and put out, a kiddie starting to whimper elsewhere, people fixing themselves for the night while a man in a long, grey coat gives out Communist leaflets, lots of praise for Uncle Joe and how they're still holding out at Stalingrad after so long. Alfred takes one because Joyce does

– except he doesn't know she's Joyce yet – and he folds it up into his pocket.

'Do you approve?'

There's this shine about her, as if she's a magazine picture, or something religious and he doesn't know why people haven't noticed and can't think why she's bothering with him – not that she truly is bothering, more like passing the time, and there's something about her that's nervous, upset, and it seems that she's speaking against her will. In those astonishing eyes there's a type of question, or a request. He can't read it exactly and maybe his want is making him find what isn't there, but he has the idea that he might be able to touch her hand and that it might calm her if he did and that he should do something to mend her: that should be his job. Of course, he'd forgotten – so tickled with his idea – that she really *had* asked him a question out loud.

'I said, do you approve? I mean, it doesn't matter if you don't.' She's dipping her words, nearly murmuring – the old dear staring sharply, trying to overhear. 'I always did think the Blimps and so on could do with getting a good old shake. We'll need things to be fairer when this is all done with, people won't stand for anything else. And we're used to sharing by this time, mucking in. And meeting each other.' She frowns at herself, at her quilt which is resting on his knees. He raises it, but she stops him. 'If you can bear to keep a hold – I've nowhere else to put it.' She glances around at the shelter, the dim, musty packing of strangers against strangers, grubby bedding, a shady fellow knocking his pipe out and laughing as if he's told an off-colour joke, elbowing his shady friend.

'Oh, God.' She gives a shiver, very small. It clatters his bones. Alfred's stomach fluttering and, 'What's wrong?' Sounding too loud to himself and not quite respectable. 'That is . . . is there something the matter?'

She shakes her head, 'No, no,' as if there was water rising to meet her and she hadn't expected it. 'Would you like a sandwich? I have some. There's spam, or there's jam. My mother made the jam. No way of telling who makes the spam – some Yank, I suppose. Oh, Lordy. You must think I'm cracked.'

Alfred wants her to stop and has cramp in his arm from needing to reach across to her, only then he wouldn't know what he should do – even if she didn't slap him – which she would – and also that aircraft recognition feeling is seeping into him again like sin. It's tearing him: trying to seem presentable and this nasty eagerness, a bad want of her that breeds more of itself and tricks his breathing up and what kind of man can he be that he likes his going wrong, loves that it springs him up, leaves him hiding his lap under her quilt.

It had a gold satin cover, her quilt, very smooth. His hands were ugly when he set them down against it. He seemed to himself a very ugly little man.

'I'm sorry. I don't know your name, Sergeant. Did I see you were a sergeant?' She turns slightly and this presses her shoulder into his, covers his stripes, strips his heart back to the breech.

Saliva so thick in his mouth that it gets in the way. 'Yes . . . I'm a very new sergeant. Air gunner.' Better be honest from the start. 'But I haven't done anything yet. They make us sergeants just for saying that we will.' Be honest in what you can.

'But you have a name, too . . .'

He looks for how she said this and she's smiling a little. The biddy in the corner almost growling, finally getting something worth her disapproval.

'Alfie, I suppose.' His voice muffled by pressing down against so much.

'Hello, Alfie you suppose.'

'Hello.'

Then a horrible silence and some kid coughing as if he's swallowed a button, or something, and the distant thump of things starting up out in the world.

'You could ask *my* name, if you wanted. As we'll be spending the night together. It's quite all right, these days. Everyone's very modern and no one comes to any harm. Not much from that, anyway.' She doesn't sound modern herself, or casual about this – more as if she's pushing into somewhere she won't like.

And now you have to make her happy, have to help and that

means you can be a good boy really, a good bad boy and that calms you. A bit. 'Well, I don't know . . . I've never been in London . . . At home we had an Anderson out the back, used that.' Understanding she'll find your old life unattractive, but you can't stop. 'Wouldn't have been any good if my sisters were still at home – not enough room – I've got a whole wing of sisters, but they left years ago – married. Apart from Nan, she's in . . .' Can't say she's in service, not with someone who probably has servants. 'I'm the youngest: the babby.' Sounding soft as shit, but it matters much less than it ought, because of how safe you seem, how well, how comfortable she makes you.

She felt like home – gave me that.

Then stole it.

And when he'd finished, finally run down, he turned and discovered her watching him, apparently pleased, but also surprised in some way – as if he had opened a door on her while she was busy with something else, a duty she didn't like.

'Sergeant Alfie, you still haven't asked me what I'm called.'

'Maybe I shouldn't.' Because he knew he had to. This feeling that he could die if he didn't know.

'I'm Joyce.'

Landing like a hot stone in him. 'Oh.' Rippling his breath, rocking what had only ever stood before, some place in himself he hadn't known. 'Hello, Joyce.'

The city outside the shelter louder now: desynchronised engines worrying in and the dull shake of bombs, ack-ack doing its best. Not a big raid, but enough.

The batteries firing up always seemed inadequate, thin. Never like that when you got on the other end of the German flak, had to ride across boxes of the bastard stuff, pretend you didn't mind.

But when you were busy, you didn't, that was the marvellous thing. It was a mercy. Like her.

He said her name again just because it tasted lovely. 'Hello, Joyce.'

'Hello, Alfie.'

His breathing all shallow and helpless, making him babble at her. 'At the back of Ma's house there was an ack-ack emplacement

– three lads and some sandbags and a Bofors gun. Ma used to bring them mugs of tea. I think everyone did.' He didn't know why he was telling her this, it wasn't the right kind of thing, not witty, intelligent, not any use. 'Then one morning after a raid, she went out to see them and their heads were lying in the lane. Blown off. There in the lane . . . She shouldn't have had to find that.' Joyce was still watching his face though, listening. Brave girl. 'I was away by then. Training.' He tried to swallow and didn't quite. 'Finished now, though. Well, the basics. Not operational, but I've got the brevet.' He wanted to shut up. 'Would you like to see?' He wanted to start again, be a man she would like.

But it truly did seem that she didn't mind him and so he angled himself to let her see his wing – and his pretty lousy sewing – while her concentration, her attention felt enormous, like a kick from Sergeant Hartnell, only deeper and wonderful, like a strange recoil echoing in his chest. He felt it, the breath when he split open.

'Alfie, I came here –' She faces straight ahead now, falters. 'Alfie.'

She is so, she is too much. She hurts him with being Joyce, even when she seems not quite concerned with him, is preoccupied. She is the first good hurt he's known.

'Alfie, I came here because I wanted to be with people, but I don't think I can stand being jammed in like this all night . . . This will sound awful . . .' She checks with him now and he shakes his head for her before he knows why and maybe she's going, maybe he's leaned up against her side too hard and she's offended and their having met is over and no more of it to come and perhaps now he has to be shaking his head because he can't let that be true.

'This will sound awful, but I don't want to go back alone.'

Alfred's mouth hasn't got a clue – his mind, likewise – they can't help him. He is beyond wanting her, lost in a splendid, shining fear.

Joyce clears her throat. 'Look, I wouldn't ask. And I also shouldn't. And you ought to know that I'm a married woman. I really am terribly married and I don't want there to be misunderstandings.'

She says other things after that, but he doesn't hear them. He thinks he might still be shaking his head, because here is something else that can't be true.

Then she is quiet, tense. He hugs the quilt. Doesn't want to give it back. Perhaps he is shaking his head about that. It would be very simple if this could be all about a quilt.

She brushes his hand, which stings, or lights, or twitches, he doesn't know which without looking and he doesn't look and she tells him, 'You really don't mind? I do realise it's an imposition.' His head still swinging back and forth without him and that blasted old woman tutting and acting as if she's outraged, when there is nothing to be outraged about.

Joyce again, insisting gently, 'Because I'd probably get out now, if we were going.'

And he stands and his legs are unhelpful and he follows Joyce, because he can't do otherwise.

Should have stayed where I was. Stayed safe.

But I couldn't.

Not in a million years.

So they'd gone out beneath the edge of the passing raid, rushed out before anyone could stop them.

He'd stumbled through the streets beside her. The moon apparently swollen, watching: at its highest and very naked, very bright for them.

Thinking all the way that what she said was one thing and how she seemed was another and you believe how someone seems, don't you? That's common sense.

The reek of fires as they went. The harsh, the sweet, the rotten: another lesson war would teach you, the way there could be such variety in waste, the infinite variations of fire.

They stepped across the head of a street, something leering at its end: a squat, red threat and a bell sounding, a fire engine going somewhere and a whistle blown, three blasts. Funny how you heard the detail and not the guns any more, not the Heinkels, not the bombs: the larger noise of that more like a grip around you, a heaviness you moved through and learned to ignore unless it pressed too sharp, came down and bit you.

Alfred saw the muffled street lights changing and pausing, showing their signals in the proper order, as if anybody cared. The scent of her quilt and of her hair were so much the only urgent things.

A little dog ran past, upset – yipping and snapping, which made Joyce draw in her breath and then what sounded like a shell fragment dropped down quite close and she held his arm. And he let her.

And they went on like that.

Otherwise, he might have said goodnight when they found her doorstep. He might have tried to.

'This is very decent of you.' She struggles with the lock in her front door while you look at nothing and her arms are pointlessly full and the glasses case drops again. 'Damn and blast the –' And there are tiny noises from her that make you think she's crying, so you rescue the case and follow her into the darkened hall of a house that smells expensive, officer class.

'Mind, there are stairs.' Something lost about her voice and you don't know this dark and so there is only her in it and your idea of her and your clinging on round the gold satin cover of a quilt. Together you rise and turn with the curve of the staircase, fumble your way.

When they reach the second landing, she's easier with her keys and another door, but she pauses in the hallway beyond. Alfred hears himself a long way away whispering, 'You didn't need to say, you know.' Whispering to Joyce. 'About being married. You never needed to say. I wouldn't do anything . . . not because I was in your house. I only . . . I'm not . . . I wouldn't have done anything.'

'I'm sorry.'

'Well, I had to tell you.'

'I'm sorry.'

'Well, I think I had to tell you that.'

And she is most likely crying again – sounds like it – and hurries off up the passageway and he hears a clattering, confusion, something heavy tipping over, but just waits, leans against the wall and puts his hand on to the paper, thinks he is touching her wall – there will always be this place where his hand was and he touched her house.

He closes the front door and the dark becomes a little darker.

He waits.

'I'm, I'm sorry.' Her voice rather distant, calling. 'You should . . .' Then a spill of light ahead and to the left, the shapes of little tables now along the corridor and a clock, door frames. Officer class. 'Do – Ah, do come in.'

For a diving moment he wonders what room she is in, because different rooms have different meanings and this will be important and he wants and does not want to know what he will be supposed to do.

'I forget if I put up the blackout and then I . . . I mean, I must have done it this time, because it was dark before I went out, but sometimes . . .'

Then he moves himself forward, lets her talk him forward.

'So I'm in this habit now. Crashing about through the dark. I broke a vase yesterday which Donald's mother liked especially . . . I . . . I'm not very good at this war. Maybe when they have another.'

And there she is in an untidy kitchen – not a bedroom, or a parlour: a kitchen – sitting at the table, wearing her coat. Her head is dropped and her fringe hides her face. There are two nice cups and saucers set out and two plates and that would be for her and for him. Her hand is holding a teaspoon, turning it over and over. There is no sugar bowl. She has perhaps forgotten it. There is a smell that is faint, but not clean, stale.

Alfred blinks. 'Do you, would you . . . This quilt.'

'Oh, my goodness. I am a BF, aren't I?' She darts up, wet-eyed, and snatches away his bundle, almost runs to another room somewhere to his right. He thinks he might sit down and, after a while, he does and holds her teaspoon and turns it over and over. No sugar bowl. No milk.

He hears when she steps back in, feels a line taut in his neck.

'There, that's . . . ' She pauses until he glances round. 'You're very kind.'

'I don't think so.'

'I think so. I think you're very kind.'

'No.'

She is a little more collected, slower – he heard water running while she was gone and imagines that she must have washed her face. Carefully, she pours him cocoa from her Thermos and takes out her sandwiches from the packet and puts them on the plates – two sandwiches each. Then she reconsiders and gives him three. It doesn't matter, because he can't eat them, can barely sip the watery cocoa.

'Don't you want to be in your basement?' Although the raid seems a good way east by this time, not their concern.

'I couldn't. I mean, sometimes I don't. I mean, there'll be my neighbours and if you're here –'

'I can leave.' Which is his first lie to her.

'No.' Which is when they look at each other.

And there is nothing to be said. And Alfred sits and believes what he sees and allows himself to be in love, cannot prevent himself being in love.

Then quietly she turns the lamp out and takes the blackout down and they stand side by side and, in the window, Alfred watches the swipes and smears of warlight, the way it searches, judders, bleeds. The night cracks and heals and cracks again, while he feels it tremble, his own lost skin taken in with the shake of everything and he sees the little garden below them apparently undisturbed, but made out of some dark metal, precisely engineered, mysterious.

In association with Costa

'The UK's leading weekly TV programme dedicated entirely to books, from contemporary to classics'.

This book gives you a glimpse inside the covers of the Costa Book Awards winners, but for insight into the minds of some of today's top authors, tune into *The Book Show* on Sky Arts Channel 267, every Thursday at 7pm.

Presented by Mariella Frostrup, the series has featured a variety of popular and acclaimed authors, plus interviews with names such as Salman Rushdie, Ian Rankin, Terry Pratchett, and Douglas Coupland. Forthcoming authors in 2008 include John Banville, Melvyn Burgess and Wendy Holden.

As well as the chance to win books donated by the interviewed authors, you'll also be able to find out what books are currently on their bedside tables, plus some of the country's top booksellers reveal their recommended picks for book clubs and a number of publishing insiders reveal the tricks of the trade to help budding writers get their work published.

THE BOOK SHOW ON SKY ARTS

In May 2007, Sky Arts' involvement in literature included sponsorship of the Guardian Hay Festival. For the first time a daily programme was broadcast from the festival under the banner of *Hay-On-Sky*, with guests as diverse as Gordon Brown, Alexander McCall Smith, Peter Falk and Vivienne Westwood. Sky Arts will feature extensive coverage again in 2008.

Sky Arts, the UK's only channel dedicated to all areas of the arts, offers a unique mix of classical music, opera, dance, jazz, rock, architecture, film, design, drama and literature, and is available in millions of Sky homes on Sky Channel 267.

As part of our commitment to literature Sky Arts is proud to work with Costa to bring *The Book Show* to new audiences.

Visit **www.skyarts.co.uk/thebookshow** for more information.